IDENTIFYING

GEMS & PRECIOUS
STONES

The new compact study guide and identifier

IDENTIFYING

GEMS & PRECIOUS
STONES

The new compact study guide and identifier

Cally Hall

736
HALL

CHARTWELL
BOOKS, INC.

A QUINTET BOOK

Published by Chartwell Books
A Division of Book Sales, Inc.
110 Enterprise Avenue
Secaucus, New Jersey 07094

This edition produced for sale in the U.S.A., its territories
and dependencies only.

ISBN 1–55521–842–3

This book was designed and produced by
Quintet Publishing Limited
6 Blundell Street
London N7 9BH

Creative Director: Richard Dewing
Designer: Stuart Walden
Project Editor: Katie Preston
Editor: Karin Fancett

Typeset in Great Britain by
Central Southern Typesetters, Eastbourne
Manufactured in Singapore by Colour Trend Pte. Ltd.
Printed in Singapore by Star Standard Industries Pte. Ltd.

Acknowledgements:
All photographs courtesy of the
Natural History Museum, London
Table on p19 courtesy of N.A.G. Press (*Famous Diamonds*,
2nd ed., by Ian Balfour)

CONTENTS

· · · · · · · · · · · · · ·

INTRODUCTION

··

The study and identification of gemstones is a fascinating and exciting topic. It is not simply a matter of looking at the stone, noting its shape and colour, and identifying it.

Being a gemmologist is rather like being a detective. Often a magnifying hand lens or microscope is needed to look closely at the stone for tell-tale clues such as inclusions or growth features. Further pieces of equipment (such as a refractometer or spectroscope) may be needed to describe how light is affected as it passes through a gemstone.

Since ancient times, gemstones have been imitated, and people have tried to recognize these fakes. Synthetic gem-quality stones have been made in laboratories since 1902 and there is continual improvement in manufacturing processes. As each new technique is introduced, the detective gemmologist has a new case to work on. The study of gemstones is therefore an ever-changing topic.

The keen amateur should not be put off by the hidden clues, for there is still much that can be recognized using the eye alone. The clear photographs throughout this book will be of value and interest to those without gemmological apparatus who wish to identify gemstones.

BEAUTY, DURABILITY AND RARITY

Gemstones have been valued throughout history for their beauty. They have been fashioned to be worn as jewellery, used to decorate objects, exquisitely carved to be admired, or collected to impress.

With the exception of organic materials such as coral and pearl, most gems are minerals that have formed within the rocks of the Earth. They have a definite chemical composition and are made up of atoms arranged in ordered patterns which result in the narrow ranges of physical and optical properties by which they may be identified.

To be considered a gemstone there are three requirements: beauty, durability and rarity. To appreciate the beauty of gemstones we need light, for it is the light and the way that it is reflected and re-fracted that causes the colour of emerald, the fire of diamond and the play of colour of opal. The skill of the cutter and polisher is necessary to reveal the full beauty of gemstones which may be found as rough pebbles or flawed crystals.

The second requirement is durability. Gemstones must be tough and hard, and resistant to chemical alteration. The German mineralogist Friedrich Mohs developed a scale to quantify the hardness of minerals. He took ten minerals and placed them in order so that each was scratched by those above it on the scale but was in turn scratched by those beneath it on the scale. The intervals in Mohs' scale are not equal. The difference in hardness between corundum (9) and diamond (10) is greater than that between corundum (9) and talc (1). For use in jewellery, gemstones must be hard enough to withstand the wear and tear of use. Most dust includes some quartz which has a hardness of about 7 on Mohs' scale; gemstones with a hardness less than 7 are therefore likely to become scratched with time.

The toughness of gemstones is related to their atomic structure. A clean break may occur along lines of atomic weakness (cleavage planes). Diamond is the hardest natural material but due to weak atomic bonding along cleavage planes it may break (cleave) if dropped or hit with a hard object. This property is often used in the early stages of preparing a diamond for cutting and polishing. Jadeite and nephrite have a structure of interlocking fibres or grains that make them the toughest gemstones even though they only have a hardness of about 7 on Mohs' scale.

When a gemstone breaks along a surface that is not a cleavage plane it is said to have fractured. Fracture may be uneven, hackly (jagged) or conchoidal (shell-like). Glass imitations of gemstones may be identified by their conchoidal fracture.

The rarity of gemstones adds to their value. Although some minerals are fairly common, gem-quality material may be exceptionally rare. Quartz is found world-wide but only a minute proportion is cuttable, whereas diamonds are rare but much is cuttable. The commercial value of gemstones depends upon their size and weight, their colour and clarity and prevailing fashion. The carat (a fifth of a gram) is the measure used to describe the weight of a gemstone.

– HARDNESS OF MINERALS AND COMMON ITEMS –

Mohs' Scale	Item	Mohs' Scale	Item	Mohs' Scale	Item
1	Talc	5	Apatite	7	Quartz
2.5	Finger nail	5.5	Glass window	8	Topaz
3	Copper coin	6	Orthoclase feldspar	9	Corundum
4	Fluorite	6.5	Steel file	10	Diamond

PROPERTIES OF GEMSTONES

STRUCTURE

Most gemstones have a crystalline structure. In crystalline materials the outward appearance of the crystal is an expression of the internal atomic structure. Well-formed crystals have flat surfaces called faces. The crystal faces and the angles between faces are directly related to the internal atomic structure. If a mineral is made up of a mass of small, poorly formed crystals such that the crystal faces cannot be distinguished, it is termed massive.

In nature it is rare to have the conditions necessary for an absolutely perfect crystal to develop. The habit of a crystal is the usual shape that a crystal takes. The habit can be described as one or more of the crystal forms defined by sets of parallel faces and their angles. Emerald is found as hexagonal prisms (see the diagram) made up of two forms. A form consists of a number of identical faces. It is termed a

BASAL PINACOID　　　**PRISM FACES**

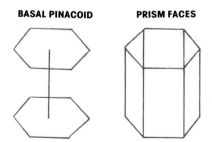

Two open forms which combine to make the hexagonal prism shape of emerald

closed form if it can enclose space or open if it cannot.

If a crystal is rotated about an imaginary straight line and the same pattern of crystal faces appears any number of times during one turn, then it is referred to as symmetrical with an axis of symmetry around the line. If the crystal appears to look the same twice during the rotation it is said to have twofold symmetry.

A crystal that has a mirror image when an imaginary line is drawn through it, is

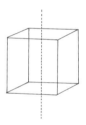

Fourfold axis of symmetry.

said to have a plane of symmetry. A crystal may have more than one plane of symmetry.

A study of the crystal shape and its symmetry enables each crystal to be assigned to one of the seven crystal symmetry systems (see table opposite).

Three of the cube's nine planes of symmetry

CLASSIFICATION	FACE SHAPE AND AXIS ORIENTATION	FORM	EXAMPLES
ISOMETRIC		All three axes are the same length and are at right angles to each other.	garnet (icositetrahedron) spinel (octahedron)
TETRAGONAL		Three axes which are at right angles to each other. The two on the same plane are equal in length while the third is perpendicular to this plane and of different length.	zircon scapolite
HEXAGONAL		Three of the four axes are in one plane and intersect at 60°. The fourth axis is perpendicular and unequal in length to the others. There are six planes of symmetry.	apatite beryl
TRIGONAL		Similar to the hexagonal system. There are three axes at 60° to each other in the same plane. The fourth axis is perpendicular. There are three planes of symmetry.	quartz sapphire
ORTHORHOMBIC		Three axes of unequal length. Two are at right angles to one another and the third is perpendicular.	peridot topaz
MONOCLINIC		There are three axes of unequal length. Two intersect at an oblique angle in one plane and the third is perpendicular.	orthoclase feldspar epidote
TRICLINIC		Three axes of unequal length all inclined to one another at different angles.	alkali feldspar (amazonite) rhodonite

REFRACTION AND REFLECTION OF LIGHT

The behaviour of light entering a crystal is dependent upon the internal atomic structure of the mineral and values for different gem minerals can be measured and used as a means of identification.

Isometric minerals and non-crystalline minerals are isotropic (have the same optical properties in all directions). When light enters them it is slowed down and its course is changed (the light ray is bent or refracted). Each ray of light is slowed down and refracted by the same amount and the mineral is said to be singly refractive. Light entering minerals crystallizing in any of the other six crystal systems (see table, page 9) is split into two rays and each ray is refracted by a different amount. These crystals are said to be doubly refractive.

Doubly refractive gemstones may appear to be different colours and different shades of the body colour when viewed from different directions. They are said to be pleochroic. Gemstones that show two colours are dichroic and belong to the tetragonal, trigonal or hexagonal crystal symmetry classes. Gemstones that show three colours are trichroic and belong to the orthorhombic, monoclinic or triclinic crystal symmetry classes. An instrument called a dichroscope can be used to see two colours side by side through the eyepiece. Stones with strong pleochroism, easily seen with the eye, include iolite (yellow, pale blue, dark blue) and tourmaline (two shades of the body colour).

*Pleochroism in an iolite cut stone. The stone shows
blue and colourless as the stone is turned.*

A cut sinhalite stone showing double refraction.

The refractive index (RI) indicates the amount that the light rays are bent by a mineral and it is measured by a refractometer. A singly refractive mineral has one refractive index but a doubly refractive mineral has a range of refractive indices. The difference between the minimum and maximum refractive indices in such a crystal is called its birefringence. When the birefringence is high the light rays can be seen to reflect off different parts of the back of the stone causing an apparent doubling of the back facets when viewed through the front facet.

The amount of light reflected at the surface of a mineral is its lustre. Most gemstones have a vitreous (glass-like) lustre. Diamond's lustre is said to be adamantine. Amber has a resinous lustre.

Light that is reflected from fibres or fibrous cavities within the mineral may appear as a cat's-eye (chatoyancy) or a star (asterism) when cut with a domed top (en cabochon). Cat's-eyes can be seen when the light is reflected from parallel arrangements of inclusions as in chrysoberyl cat's-eyes. Star stones are seen when several sets of parallel fibres reflect light. A four-rayed star has two sets of parallel fibres and a six-rayed star has three sets of parallel fibres. Occasionally a twelve-rayed sapphire star stone can be cut.

Chrysoberyl cat's-eyes or chatoyants.

COLOUR

When white light, made up of all the spectral colours, travels through a gemstone some of the colours may be absorbed within the crystal structure. The colours that do emerge combine to give the colour of the gemstone. If no part of the spectrum is absorbed the crystal will appear colourless. The "absorption spectrum" produced when white light passes through a gemstone can be viewed using an instrument called a spectroscope. Dark lines are seen in the part of the spectrum that has been absorbed by the stone. The spectroscope may be used to distinguish between stones of similar colour. A ruby coloured by chromium and a red almandine garnet coloured by iron may look the same but each has a distinctive absorption spectrum.

A gemstone viewed in white light may appear to be one colour but viewing it through a coloured filter may reveal underlying colours which can help to identify the stone. A Chelsea colour filter, for example, cuts out all of the spectrum except red and green light and through the filter a true emerald appears red while imitation emeralds appear green. The appearance under ultraviolet light and X-rays can also aid identification.

Gemstone colour may be enhanced by oiling or staining. Heat treatment or irradiation can produce colour changes, although these may fade with time.

A group including amber, ruby, ivory, fluorite and opal photographed in white and ultraviolet light.

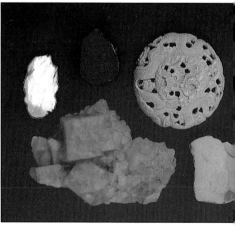

The absorption spectrum of zircon.

The ability of a gemstone to split white light into the colours of the spectrum is called dispersion. It is usually measured by finding the difference in refractive index of the stone for a red ray, which is refracted least, and a blue ray which is refracted most. Diamond has a dispersion of 0.044 which is high enough to give a good display of the spectral colours, its "fire". The degree of fire is dependent upon the body colour, clarity and facet angles.

MAGNETISM

Some minerals are magnetic and this property can be used to identify gemstones of similar colour, for example. Pyrope garnet is moderately magnetic and can be separated from non-magnetic red spinel. Sinhalite is only weakly magnetic and so can be differentiated from brown peridot, which is moderately magnetic. The table lists other gemstones and their relative magnetic properties.

– GEMSTONES – WITH HIGH DISPERSION

Mineral name	Dispersion
Cubic zirconia	0.065
Demantoid garnet	0.057
Sphene	0.051
Benitoite	0.046
Diamond	0.044
Zircon	0.039

– MAGNETIC – GEMSTONES

Magnetism	Stone
STRONG	Almandine garnet
	Spessartine garnet
	Rhodochrosite
	Rhodonite
MODERATE	Demantoid garnet
	Peridot
	Pyrope garnet
	Dark green tourmaline
	Hessonite garnet
WEAK	Brown sinhalite
	Green tourmaline

SPECIFIC GRAVITY

Specific gravity (density) is a measure of the way the atoms of the atomic structure are packed together. Specific gravity is defined as the ratio of the weight of the mineral compared to an equal volume of water. Minerals with high values of specific gravity have atoms packed tightly together. Where there are two specimens of equal size, the specimen with higher specific gravity will feel the heaviest.

FASHIONING

Gemstones may be found as rough crystals or rolled pebbles. They are cut and polished by lapidaries whose aim is to make the stone as attractive as possible while retaining as much of the weight of the stone as they can.

When deciding how best to cut a gemstone, the lapidary must have a knowledge of the properties of the stone being dealt with. Lapidaries must be aware of the stone's strengths (including hardness, dispersion "fire" and birefringence) and weaknesses (cleavage), and must carefully observe the stone for any flaws or inclusions. It is important to orientate the stone so that the best colour of a pleochroic stone is seen and flaws or inclusions are hidden.

The oldest and simplest cuts are cabochons. A stone cut *en cabochon* has a smooth polished surface with a rounded or curved outline. The cabochon cut is used mainly for opaque or translucent stones, for stones with a strong body colour, iridescence or sheen, or to show cat's-eyes or star stones to best advantage.

A collection of star-stone and cat's-eye cabochons.

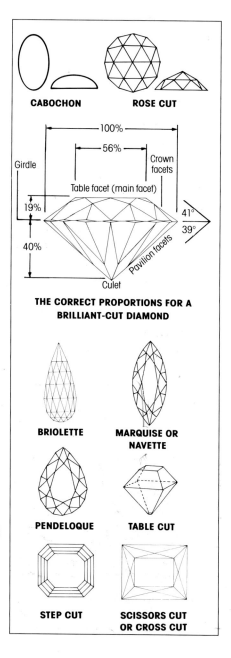

CABOCHON   ROSE CUT

THE CORRECT PROPORTIONS FOR A
BRILLIANT-CUT DIAMOND

BRIOLETTE   MARQUISE OR
NAVETTE

PENDELOQUE   TABLE CUT

STEP CUT   SCISSORS CUT
OR CROSS CUT

Transparent stones are cut to show a number of flat polished faces (faceted).

The brilliant cut is one of the most popular and is ideal for diamonds as it makes the most of the high dispersion and adamantine lustre. In an ideal cut, all the light that reaches or enters a stone is reflected. The facets at the front of the stone (crown facets) reflect light off the surface, seen as the lustre. The large central facet on the crown is the table facet. Light that enters the stone is reflected off the back facets (pavilion facets) to show the colour and fire. If the angles are not correct, some light may be lost through the back facets.

The step cut (or trap cut) has been developed for stones where the colour is the most important feature. The step-cut style of faceting is used for emeralds and rubies. There are a number of other cuts, some of which are illustrated. A rare or interesting stone may be fashioned in an unusual cut to add to its interest or to keep as much weight as possible.

Dispersion and light in (from left to right): strontium titanate, cubic zirconia, diamond, yttrium aluminium garnet (YAG) and synthetic white sapphire.

IMITATIONS

A number of different materials can be used to copy or imitate gemstones. These imitations may be man-made or natural.

Imitations may simply be pieces of glass coloured to look like gems, or they may be more complex and made up of several different materials (composite stones). The bubbles and swirls characteristic of paste may be seen even without the help of a hand lens, and scratches on the surface of the glass are often apparent. Glass is singly refractive and many of the stones it imitates are doubly refractive.

– DIAMOND – IMITATIONS

Imitation	In comparison with diamond
Spinel	less fire than diamond
Sapphire	less brilliant
YAG	heavy, lacks fire
Sphene	soft, birefringence too strong
Synthetic scheelite	soft
High zircon	birefringence too strong
Cubic zirconia	heavy
Strontium titanate	soft, more fire than diamond
Synthetic rutile	strongly birefringent, excess fire
Paste	soft
Rock crystal	lacks fire

The garnet-topped doublet was regularly used in Victorian times to imitate gemstones of various colours. These were made by cementing a piece of almandine garnet on top of a piece of glass; the garnet and glass together was then faceted to imitate ruby, sapphire or emerald. The join between the two pieces can often be seen in the top part of the stone and the difference in lustre between the parts is usually distinctive.

Soudé emeralds are composite stones made to imitate emerald by cementing two pieces of pale beryl or rock crystal together with a green cement. The junction is often concealed in a closed setting. Other composite stones include opal doublets and triplets.

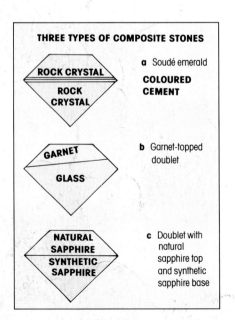

THREE TYPES OF COMPOSITE STONES

ROCK CRYSTAL
ROCK CRYSTAL
a Soudé emerald
COLOURED CEMENT

GARNET
GLASS
b Garnet-topped doublet

NATURAL SAPPHIRE
SYNTHETIC SAPPHIRE
c Doublet with natural sapphire top and synthetic sapphire base

SYNTHETICS

Synthetic stones are man-made materials that have the same chemical composition and therefore almost the same physical and optical properties as the naturally formed gemstone. Synthetics are made in laboratories using a number of techniques which include melting or dissolving powdered chemicals and then allowing them to cool and crystallize.

Synthetic corundum has characteristic internal features that may be seen using a hand lens or a microscope. Curved growth lines (instead of the straight growth lines of natural corundum) and inclusions of small bubbles can be used to help distinguish between natural and synthetic stones. Synthetic emeralds also have distinctive inclusions, including liquid-filled cavities and two-phase inclusions (a liquid and a gaseous bubble).

Pierre Gilson produced black and white opals with a structure similar to that of natural opal and giving the same play of colour. Under a microscope the Gilson opals have a distinctive mosaic pattern with a "lizard skin" appearance. Gilson synthetic turquoise can be recognized by its characteristic structure of dark blue angular particles on a whitish background. Gilson synthetic lapis lazuli can be distinguished from natural lapis lazuli by its low density and high porosity.

HOW TO USE THIS BOOK

The gemstones in the identifier section are listed in the following order:

MAIN GEM GROUPINGS, EG CORUNDUMS, GARNETS, BERYLS

OTHER PRECIOUS STONES

NATURAL GLASSES

ORGANICS

To find the reference to a specific gem or precious stone, refer to the index at the back of the book.

– KEY TO SYMBOLS –

Each identifier entry has information on:

CRYSTAL STRUCTURE

 isometric

 orthorhombic

 tetragonal

 monoclinic

 hexagonal

 triclinic

 trigonal

 amorphous

REFRACTIVE INDEX

 singly refractive

 doubly refractive

Birefringence if stone is doubly refractive

SPECIFIC GRAVITY

HARDNESS ON MOHS' SCALE

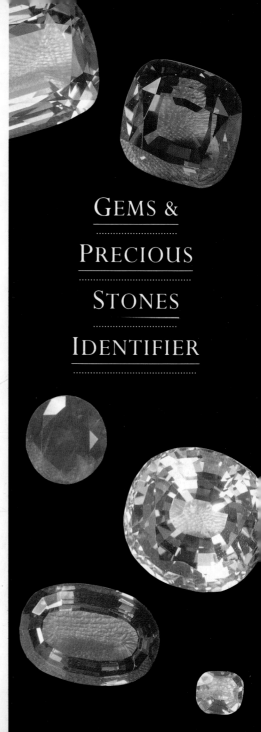

GEMS &
PRECIOUS
STONES
IDENTIFIER

DIAMOND

CHEMICAL COMPOSITION: CARBON

Most gem diamonds are white (colourless). Diamonds with a strong body colour, such as brown, yellow, pink, red, blue or green are known as fancy diamonds. The name "diamond" is derived from the Greek *adamas* meaning unconquerable.

PHYSICAL AND OPTICAL PROPERTIES

Diamond crystals form as cubes, octahedra and dodecahedra, the octahedra being the form most commonly used for gems. Diamond has an adamantine lustre and very good "fire" (dispersion), which makes it the most popular gemstone.

The bluish-white fluorescence of most diamonds under ultraviolet light is used in identification. Colourless to yellow diamonds which show a blue fluorescence and have the strongest absorption line in the violet part of the spectrum are members of the Cape series. Other diamonds may show a green or yellow glow under ultraviolet light and have absorption lines in other parts of the spectrum.

LOCALITIES AND ROCK TYPES

The ancient diamond mines in the Golconda area of southern India have been the source of some of the most famous diamonds such as the Koh-i-nor and Jehangir. Diamond is widespread in Brazil and most gems, although small, are of good quality. Carbonado is an unusual black microcrystalline diamond found in river gravels in Bahia, Brazil. Ballas (boart) is another important type of industrial diamond found in Brazil and South Africa.

Alluvial diamonds have been found in almost every state of the USA and the largest north American diamond (weighing 40.23 carats) was found in a now abandoned mine at Murfreesboro, Arkansas. Until recently Australian diamonds were small and yellowish, but white and fancy-coloured stones, such as pink and pinkish-brown, are now mined at Argyle in the Kimberley district of northern Western Australia. Probably the most famous diamond bearing country is South Africa. The first diamond was reported in 1866. In 1869 the Star of South Africa was found weighing 83.5 carats and later cut into a pear-shaped brilliant weighing 47.74 carats. Other localities include Borneo, Botswana, China, Ghana, Guinea, Guyana, Russia, Tanzania, Venezuela, Zaire and Zimbabwe.

FASHIONING, IMITATIONS AND SYNTHETICS

Diamonds are usually cut in the brilliant style which has proportions calculated to show the diamond at its best by ensuring as much light as possible entering the stone is reflected back through the front facet.

Diamonds have been imitated by many colourless minerals and also by glass. The fire of diamond is distinctive, and the ability of diamond to conduct heat can be used to identify it using a conductivity meter. Diamonds suitable for industrial use have been made synthetically since 1954, but gem-quality diamond was not made until 1970 and is rarely used as a gemstone.

SPECIFIC GRAVITY 3.52   **HARDNESS** 10   CRYSTAL SYSTEM **ISOMETRIC**   SINGLY REFRACTIVE **2.42**

– THE WORLD'S LARGEST DIAMONDS –

THE WORLD'S LARGEST ROUGH DIAMONDS

Rank	Carats	Name	Discovery date	Place	Cut into
1	3,106.00	CULLINAN	1905	South Africa	Cullinans I-IX; 96 others
2	995.20	EXCELSIOR	1893	South Africa	21 gems (largest 69.80)
3	968.90	STAR OF S. LEONE	1972	Sierra Leone	–
4	890.00	THE INCOMPARABLE	1984	Zale Corp.	Incomparable; 14 others
5	770.00	WOYIE RIVER	1945	Sierra Leone	30 gems (largest 31.35)
6	755.50	UNNAMED BROWN	1984	South Africa	Unnamed Brown
7	726.60	VARGAS	1938	Brazil	Vargas (48.26); 22 others
8	726.00	JONKER	1934	South Africa	Jonker (125.65); 11 others
9	650.25	REITZ	1895	South Africa	Jubilee (245.35); one other
10	609.25	BAUMGOLD ROUGH	1923	South Africa	14 gems (sizes unknown)

THE WORLD'S LARGEST CUT DIAMONDS

Rank	Carats	Name	Colour	Shape	Last reported owner or location
1	545.67	UNNAMED BROWN	dark brown	fire-rose	De Beers Consolidated Mines Ltd
2	530.20	CULLINAN I	white	pear	British Crown Jewels – Tower of London
3	407.48	INCOMPARABLE	brownish yellow	triolette	Auctioned in New York, October 1988
4	317.40	CULLINAN II	white	cushion	British Crown Jewels – Tower of London
5	277.00	NIZAM	white	dome	Nizam of Hyderabad – 1934
6	273.85	CENTENARY	white	modified heart	De Beers Consolidated Mines Ltd
7	245.35	JUBILEE	white	cushion	Paul-Louis Weiller
8	234.50	DE BEERS	light yellow	cushion	Auctioned in Geneva, May 1982
9	205.07	RED CROSS	yellow	square brilliant	Auctioned in Geneva, November 1973
10	202.00	BLACK STAR OF AFRICA	black	–	Exhibited in Tokyo, 1971

RUBY

CORUNDUM GROUP
CHEMICAL COMPOSITION: ALUMINIUM OXIDE

Rubies are a form of corundum. Pure corundum is colourless and the gem colour is caused by the presence of small amounts of chemical impurities. Small traces of chromium give rise to the rich red colour of ruby – the name is derived from the Latin for red, *ruber*. If there is any brown hue in the stone it is due to the presence of iron impurities.

PHYSICAL AND OPTICAL PROPERTIES

Ruby crystallizes in the trigonal crystal system, but the habit varies with the variety and locality, for example Burmese rubies are usually found as tabular (flat) hexagonal prisms terminated at both ends. Ruby has an uneven or conchoidal (shell-like) fracture. There is no true cleavage but a line of weakness or parting may be present. The lustre is vitreous.

The absorption spectrum is characterized by fine lines in the red, lines which cut out most of the yellow, most of the green and violet parts of the spectrum. When rubies are viewed through "crossed filters" (the stone is placed in a beam of light which has passed through a flask of blue copper sulphate solution and is then viewed through a chelsea colour filter), the chromium causes a luminescence that can be seen as a red glow.

LOCALITIES AND ROCK TYPES

The highest quality rubies come from the Mogok area of Burma. Written records of ruby mining go back as far as 1597, but legends tell of mining long before. Gems are also collected from river gravels. The colour of the best Burmese stones is described as "pigeon's blood". Thailand provides most of the world's rubies, but they are a brownish-red and darker in

colour than the Burmese rubies. Rubies from Tanzania are distinctive as they are found as short prismatic crystals in a bright green rock. Rubies have been found in mica schists in the Hunza Valley in Pakistan that are up to 2in/5cm in length. Small quantities are also found in Afghanistan, Australia, Brazil, Cambodia, Mysore in India, Malawi and the USA (Montana and North Carolina).

FASHIONING, IMITATIONS AND SYNTHETICS

Rubies are faceted or cut en cabochon. Stones may have inclusions of the

mineral rutile. These appear as short needle-like shapes arranged within the crystal in lines parallel with the edges of the crystal. This may be seen as a sheen known as "silk" or cut en cabochon to show a six-pointed star.

Rubies were first made synthetically towards the end of the 19th century using the flame-fusion method. They soon became the first gems to be made in commercial quantities. Sythetic rubies have replaced the "jewel" rubies which were traditionally used as bearings in watches and precision instruments.

| SPECIFIC GRAVITY 4.0 | HARDNESS 9.0 | CRYSTAL SYSTEM **TRIGONAL** | DOUBLY REFRACTIVE **1.76–1.78** | BIREFRINGENCE **0.008** |

SAPPHIRE

CORUNDUM GROUP
CHEMICAL COMPOSITION: ALUMINIUM OXIDE

The name sapphire is given to any colour of corundum other than red, the red stones being rubies. Although sapphires are commonly thought of as being blue and the name is derived from the Greek *sapphirus* for blue, they can be black, purple, violet, dark blue, bright blue, light blue, green, yellow and orange. The blue colours are due to traces of titanium and iron and the red hues are due to chromium.

PHYSICAL AND OPTICAL PROPERTIES

As with ruby, sapphires crystallize in the trigonal crystal system and the form the crystals take depends on the variety and locality, for example Sri Lankan sapphires are usually found as bipyramids. Sapphires have an uneven or shell-like fracture, but no real cleavage. They have a glass-like (vitreous) lustre.

LOCATIONS AND ROCK TYPES

Burmese sapphires are of excellent quality. The stones are found in a coarse yellow sand and often have feather-like inclusions. Colour is important in determining the origin of a stone; cornflower blue sapphires from Kashmir occur in pegmatite rock and as water-worn pebbles in river valleys. The colours of Sri Lankan sapphires include pale blue, violet, yellow, white, green and pink and the rare orange-pink sapphire called *padparadscha*, which comes from a Sinhalese word meaning "lotus-colour". Blue, green and yellow corundum is found in Queensland and New South Wales, Australia. Australian sapphires are usually rather dark blue and somewhat inky but there is an attractive greenish-yellow variety. Other localities include Brazil, Burma, Cambodia, Kenya, Malawi, Tanzania, Thailand and Zimbabwe.

FASHIONING, IMITATIONS AND SYNTHETICS

Sapphire is often parti-coloured (one part is blue and the rest is colourless). The cutter places the clear part near the front of the gem and blue part towards the back so that the complete stone appears blue from the front. Stones are usually faceted as mixed cut gems. Star-stones are cut en cabochon. Corundums are imitated by spinel, garnet and glass. A garnet-topped doublet, with a blue glass base and a garnet top may imitate sapphire. Most of the blue glasses and blue doublets show strong red through the Chelsea colour filter and can be distinguished from real sapphires which do not. A quartz cabochon with coloured reflective pieces on its base may be used to imitate star corundum.

| SPECIFIC GRAVITY 4.0 | HARDNESS 9.0 | | CRYSTAL SYSTEM **TRIGONAL** | | DOUBLY REFRACTIVE **1.76–1.78** | BIREFRINGENCE **0.008** |

EMERALD

BERYL GROUP
CHEMICAL COMPOSITION: BERYLLIUM ALUMINIUM SILICATE

Emerald is the best-known variety of beryl and is green in colour. The colour is due to a trace of chromium and usually some iron. The name emerald is derived from the Greek *smaragdus*, which in turn was derived from an earlier Persian word meaning a green mineral. Cleopatra's emerald mine by the Red Sea in Egypt dates back to about 2000BC and was probably the source of most of the emerald used in ancient jewellery.

PHYSICAL AND OPTICAL PROPERTIES
Emerald crystallizes as hexagonal prisms with two flat terminations. Occasionally, small pyramidal faces bevel the junction of the flat (basal) face and the prism faces. There is poor cleavage parallel to the basal plane. Lustre is vitreous.
Emerald has distinct dichroism, showing blue-green and yellowish-green. Most emeralds show bright red through the Chelsea colour filter. In South African and Indian stones this fluorescence is dulled by the presence of iron and they may show green through the filter.

LOCALITIES AND ROCK TYPES
The world's finest emeralds are from the Chivor and Muzo mines in Colombia. The crystals are found in cracks or pockets within the rock. Chivor stones usually show a strong red under the Chelsea colour filter and a red fluorescence under ultraviolet light. Three-phase inclusions are typical. Beautiful yellowish-green emeralds, often with three-phase inclusions (containing sodium chloride – common salt), are found in the Muzo mines. The colour of emerald and the inclusions

within it may give clues as to its source. Emeralds from the Bahia and Minas Gerais regions of Brazil are of a pale yellowish-green colour and are coloured by chromium. They are fairly clear but may contain two-phase inclusions. Emeralds are found in the Ekaterinburg region of Russia, but the larger stones are generally cloudy. Australian emeralds are mainly pale and badly flawed and often embedded in other minerals. The larger emerald crystals found in South Africa are also usually cloudy or flawed and typically contain brown mica plate inclusions. Zimbabwean emeralds from the Sandawana area are a superb green; they are commonly zoned and have inclusions of tremolite needles or rods. Indian emeralds vary in quality and have characteristic "comma" inclusions (oblong cavities containing a liquid and a bubble of gas). Other localities include the Habachtal area of Austria, Norway, Pakistan, Tanzania, the USA and Zambia.

FASHIONING, IMITATIONS AND SYNTHETICS
The best-quality emeralds are cut in the trap-cut or step-cut style, also known as the emerald cut. Emerald that is flawed but has a good colour may be carved. Poor-quality flawed emeralds are cut en cabochon or as beads. Almost all emeralds are oiled to fill cracks and improve their appearance.
Composites, such as garnet-topped doublets, soudé emeralds, composites using quartz, or spinel or glass are used to imitate emerald. Sometimes pale emeralds are painted or foiled on the back to improve their colour. Crackled quartz dyed green is sometimes called "Indian emerald". Most imitations of emerald show green through the Chelsea colour filter.
Synthetic emeralds were first produced just before World War II, and have since been made in commercial quantities in the USA and elsewhere. Early synthetic emeralds show a red colour through the Chelsea colour filter that is far brighter than that from natural emerald.

SPECIFIC GRAVITY 2.71   **HARDNESS** 7.5

 CRYSTAL SYSTEM **HEXAGONAL**

 DOUBLY REFRACTIVE **1.57**

BIREFRINGENCE **0.006**

AQUAMARINE

BERYL GROUP
CHEMICAL COMPOSITION: BERYLLIUM ALUMINIUM SILICATE

Aquamarine is a blue-green variety of beryl. The best quality aquamarine has a sky-blue colour. The name aquamarine means sea water.

PHYSICAL AND OPTICAL PROPERTIES

Hexagonal crystals of aquamarine are often large and flawless. They may be striated, making them like a ribbed cylinder, and tapered due to erosion. Lustre is vitreous and there is a weak basal cleavage.
Aquamarine is dichroic showing colourless and deep blue. The absorption spectrum is weak and there is no luminescence. A strong greenish-blue colour is seen through the Chelsea colour filter. Some aquamarines show chatoyancy (the cat's-eye effect) when cut en cabochon.

LOCALITIES AND ROCK TYPES

The best known locality for gem quality aquamarine is Minas Gerais, Brazil where crystals have been weathered out from pegmatites and are found as alluvial deposits in a layer of brown gravel called Cascalho. The Russian Urals are also known for their fine aquamarine. There are said to be 50 sources of beryl, including aquamarine, on the island of Madagascar. Aquamarine is found in Burma but is not common in Sri Lanka. Other localities include Argentina, China, India, Namibia, Northern Ireland, Norway, . Tanzania, the USA and Zimbabwe.

FASHIONING, IMITATOINS AND SYNTHETICS

The cutter normally uses a trap-cut on aquamarine because of the pale colour. The size of the stone is kept large enough to give a fairly strong colour and

the table facet is cut parallel to the length of the prismatic crystals to get maximum colour. The blue colour is usually enhanced by heat treatment.
Aquamarine is imitated by synthetic spinel coloured with cobalt. The imitation can be recognized because it appears bright red through the Chelsea

colour filter (instead of green). Pale blue glass imitating aquamarine is easily recognized as it is only singly refractive, whereas aquamarine is doubly refractive. Topaz may look similar to aquamarine, but the refractometer will show the higher refractive index readings of topaz.

| SPECIFIC GRAVITY 2.69 | HARDNESS 7.5 | | CRYSTAL SYSTEM HEXAGONAL | | DOUBLY REFRACTIVE 1.57 | BIREFRINGENCE 0.006 |

MORGANITE

BERYL GROUP
CHEMICAL COMPOSITION: BERYLLIUM ALUMINIUM SILICATE

PHYSICAL AND OPTICAL PROPERTIES
The pink, rose and peach colours of morganite are due to manganese.

Morganite is heat treated to drive off any yellow tinge and so enhance the colour. It is named after J P Morgan, an American banker and gem enthusiast. Morganite is usually found as tabular prisms. It is dichroic, the two colours being pink and a deeper bluish-pink. There is no characteristic absorption spectrum and luminescence under ultraviolet light is weak. Under X-rays there is an intense red glow.

LOCALITIES AND ROCK TYPES
A pure pink morganite is found in Minas Gerais, Brazil and also in Madagascar. Pale rose-coloured beryl is found around San Diego, California (USA). Deposits also occur in Mozambique, Namibia and Zimbabwe.

FASHIONING, IMITATIONS AND SYNTHETICS
Morganite is usually facetd as trap-cut stones in order to give a strong colour. Morganite is imitated by pink topaz, kunzite, natural and synthetic pink sapphire and spinel. Garnet-topped doublets and pastes are also made in a pink colour.

SPECIFIC GRAVITY 2.80	HARDNESS 7.5	CRYSTAL SYSTEM **HEXAGONAL**	DOUBLY REFRACTIVE **1.60**	BIREFRINGENCE **0.008**

HELIODOR

BERYL GROUP
CHEMICAL COMPOSITION: BERYLLIUM ALUMINIUM SILICATE

PHYSICAL AND OPTICAL PROPERTIES
Heliodor varies in colour from a pale yellow to a rich golden colour. The name heliodor is derived from the Greek meaning sun and gift. Its physical properties are like those of aquamarine. The absorption spectrum is weak and the presence of iron, which gives rise to the golden-yellow colour, dulls any luminescence. Although many heliodors, morganites and aquamarines are virtually flawless, inclusions in the form of slender, parallel tubes can occur which reduce the stones' transparency and lustre.

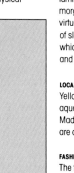

LOCALTIES AND ROCK TYPES
Yellow beryls are found in all the aquamarine localities, particularly Madagascar, Brazil and Namibia. They are also found in the USA (Connecticut).

FASHIONING, IMITATIONS AND SYNTHETICS
The trap cut is the most usual cut for yellow beryls as they need the depth to give a strong colour.

SPECIFIC GRAVITY 2.68	HARDNESS 7.5	CRYSTAL SYSTEM **HEXAGONAL**	DOUBLY REFRACTIVE **1.57**	BIREFRINGENCE **0.005**

– OTHER VARIETIES OF BERYL –

Dark brown beryl has a bronzy sheen, which is due to inclusions of the mineral ilmenite. It shows a star when cut en cabochon. This type of beryl is found at Minas Gerais, Brazil.

Red beryl, or bixbite, is a relatively highly valued gemstone. This is due to its rarity, distinctive colours and its only recent discovery. The stones have a strong ruby-red, violet or strawberry-red colour. The small crystals contain many inclusions and are often internally flawed. Red beryl is found in the USA (New Mexico and Utah).

ROCK CRYSTAL

QUARTZ GROUP
CHEMICAL COMPOSITION: SILICA

Rock crystal derives its name from the Greek *krustallos* meaning ice. The Greeks believed that colourless quartz was ice that had been frozen by the Gods and would never thaw.

PHYSICAL AND OPTICAL PROPERTIES
Rock crystal is found as hexagonal prisms which are characterized by horizontal striations on the prism faces and it has a vitreous lustre. Twinning is common and some crystals are doubly terminated. There is no distinct cleavage and fracture is conchoidal. Rock crystal is often clear, but if there are inclusions they are usually two-phase (a crystal-shaped cavity containing a crystal or liquid and a bubble of gas). "Venus hair stone" or "needle stone" are names given to rutilated quartz. Tourmalinated quartz has inclusions of crystals of black tourmaline. These may be cut en cabochon or faceted. "Rainbow quartz" or "iris quartz" is rock crystal that has

cracks which produce the colours of the rainbow due to interference of light at the thin films of air in the cracks. Rock crystal is transparent to ultraviolet rays, as is all quartz.

LOCALITIES AND ROCK TYPES
Rock crystal is found all over the world, and is, in fact, one of the most commonly occurring minerals in the Earth's crust. Good crystals are found in the Swiss and French Alps, but the most important locality is Brazil.

FASHIONING, IMITATIONS AND SYNTHETICS
Rock crystal has been used as faceted stones and beads and in composite stones, to imitate other gemstones. Carvings and engraved pieces were first made by the ancient Greeks and it is still carved, particularly in Germany. Flat rock crystal beads (rondels) are often used to separate coloured stones. Rock crystal may be imitated by glass, but can be distinguished from glass by its birefringence and unlike glass it does not contain air bubbles.

| SPECIFIC GRAVITY 2.65 | HARDNESS 7.0 | CRYSTAL SYSTEM **TRIGONAL** | DOUBLY REFRACTIVE **1.54–1.55** | BIREFRINGENCE **0.009** |

– BIRTHSTONES –

Month	Colour	Official stone	Month	Colour	Official stone
January	Dark red	Garnet	July	Red	Ruby
February	Purple	Amethyst	August	Pale green	Peridot
March	Pale blue	Aquamarine	September	Deep blue	Sapphire
April	White (transparent)	Diamond	October	Variegated	Opal
May	Bright green	Emerald	November	Yellow	Topaz
June	Cream	Pearl	December	Sky-blue	Turquoise

Decorative box set with a large citrine and other gemstones. A lizard carved in cat's-eye quartz.

– ELECTRICAL PROPERTIES OF QUARTZ –

Quartz exhibits a piezo-electric effect, which means that an electric charge can be induced in the crystal when pressure is applied to the crystal in certain directions. In 1922 W G Cady found that the electrically vibrating crystals could be used as a means of measuring and controlling the frequencies of radio waves. Since then many other uses of this property have been found including the use of quartz in clocks and watches, underwater signalling and detecting apparatus and as lenses in microscopes, which also takes advantage of the fact that quartz is transparent to ultraviolet rays.

AMETHYST

QUARTZ GROUP
CHEMICAL COMPOSITION: SILICA

Amethyst varies in colour from pale violet to dark purple and may be parti-coloured with clear or yellow quartz. The tips of the crystals are often darkest and may grade to colourless quartz. Amethyst is found lining hollow cavities in rocks.

PHYSICAL AND OPTICAL PROPERTIES

Amethyst changes colour with heat and stones from different localities show different colour changes to brown, yellow and sometimes green. However, these changes are unpredictable and the colour may fade. Amethyst has distinct dichroism, showing a bluish-purple and a reddish-purple. This distinguishes it from heat-treated stones which do not show any dichroism. Amethyst does not have a characteristic absorption spectrum. Inclusions are usually feather-like, or may resemble a thumb print or tiger stripes.

LOCALITIES AND ROCK TYPES

The Ural Mountains of Russia have been the main source of a reddish-coloured amethyst. Other good sources include Germany, Namibia, Western Australia and Zambia. Brazilian and Uruguayan amethyst is found in cavities in igneous rocks. Amethyst is found in a number of states in the USA, with large crystals from North Carolina and Maine. Violet-coloured amethyst is found in Canada and many geodes containing amethyst are found in the Deccan trap area of India. Good quality amethyst comes from the Sri Lankan gem gravels.

FASHIONING, IMITATIONS AND SYNTHETICS

Crystals of amethyst are cut in the mixed-cut style or the trap-cut style and are often fashioned into beads. Synthetic corundum and glass can be made in a colour to imitate amethyst. Pale amethyst has been mounted in a closed setting with paint or foil behind the stone to enhance the colour.

| SPECIFIC GRAVITY 2.65 | HARDNESS 7.0 | | CRYSTAL SYSTEM **TRIGONAL** | | DOUBLY REFRACTIVE **1.54–1.55** | BIREFRINGENCE **0.009** |

CITRINE

QUARTZ GROUP
CHEMICAL COMPOSITION: SILICA

PHYSICAL AND OPTICAL PROPERTIES
The distinctive colour of citrine is due to the presence of iron and varies from pure yellow, dull yellow, honey or brownish yellow. Citrine is dichroic but has no characteristic absorption spectrum or fluorescence. The crystals will turn white if heated and dark brown if exposed to X-rays. As with amethysts, citrines are often parti-coloured. Cut crystals have a good lustre. Larger citrine crystals take the form of prisms with pyramid ends.

LOCALITIES AND ROCK TYPES
Citrine is rare, but does occur in Brazil, France, Madagascar and the USA (Colorado).

FASHIONING, IMITATIONS AND SYNTHETICS
Faceted cuts are used for fine transparent citrines, while the remaining varieties are cut as cabochons.
Natural yellow citrine is rare and most commercial stones are actually heat-treated amethysts. Some heat-treated stones have a red tint and show no pleochroism. Citrine is used to imitate the more expensive gemstone, topaz.

SPECIFIC GRAVITY 2.65	HARDNESS 7.0		CRYSTAL SYSTEM **TRIGONAL**		DOUBLY REFRACTIVE **1.54–1.55**	BIREFRINGENCE **0.009**

BROWN QUARTZ

QUARTZ GROUP
CHEMICAL COMPOSITION: SILICA

PHYSICAL AND OPTICAL PROPERTIES
Brown quartz varies in colour from yellow-brown cairngorm, named after the Cairngorm mountains in the Scottish Highlands, and grey smoky quartz to the almost black quartz sometimes called morion. Morion can be heat treated to lighten its colour and make a more attractive stone. The smoky variety is thought to be rock crystal which has been irradiated.
Brown quartz is found as hexagonal prisms. It has no characteristic absorption spectrum or luminescence under ultraviolet light or X-rays. Brown quartz may have inclusions of the mineral rutile (titanium oxide). These are long needle-like crystals which may be seen easily without magnification. The inclusions may add to the beauty and interest of the stone.

LOCALITIES AND ROCK TYPES
The main localites for brown quartz are in the Swiss Alps. Good crystals of smoky quartz are found in Pike's Peak, Colorado (USA). Other localities include Australia, Japan and Spain.

FASHIONING, IMITATIONS AND SYNTHETICS
Brown quartz is often faceted for gemstones or carved for objets d'arts.
Most of the cairngorm variety of brown quartz is Brazilian amethyst that has been heat treated to give the brown colour.

SPECIFIC GRAVITY 2.65	HARDNESS 7.0		CRYSTAL SYSTEM **TRIGONAL**		DOUBLY REFRACTIVE **1.54–1.55**	BIREFRINGENCE **0.009**

ROSE QUARTZ

QUARTZ GROUP
CHEMICAL COMPOSITION: SILICA

PHYSICAL AND OPTICAL PROPERTIES

Rose quartz varies in colour from pale whitish-pink to dark rose pink. Magnesium and titanium have both been suggested as the impurity which causes the colour. Transparent rose quartz is very rare and the stones are usually rather cloudy. The crystals are brittle and often cracked. The stones tend to lose their colour when heated and turn black when exposed to radiation. Dichroism is apparent in the darker coloured stones.

LOCALITIES AND ROCK TYPES

Quality rose quartz is found in Brazil,

Madagascar and the USA (California and Maine).

FASHIONING, IMITATIONS AND SYNTHETICS

Some rose quartz contains tiny rutile needles which cause a star effect. This is

best seen when the stone is cut en cabochon and light is directed up through the stone. Rose quartz may be faceted although it is more usually fashioned as cabochons, beads or carved for ornaments.

SPECIFIC GRAVITY 2.65	HARDNESS 7.0		CRYSTAL SYSTEM **TRIGONAL**		DOUBLY REFRACTIVE **1.54–1.55**	BIREFRINGENCE **0.009**

MILKY QUARTZ

QUARTZ GROUP
CHEMICAL COMPOSITION: SILICA

PHYSICAL AND OPTICAL PROPERTIES

Milky quartz is of variable opacity, white and may be layered or striped with milky bands. The distinctive coloration of milky quartz is due to inclusions of numerous bubbles of gas and liquid in the crystal.

LOCALITIES AND ROCK TYPES

Milky quartz is found in pegmatites and hydrothermal veins; it is still not known exactly how the crystal forms. This variety of quartz is one of the most common materials found in the Earth's surface. Massive crystals have been found in Siberia. Other localities include

central Europe, Brazil, Madagascar, Namibia and the USA.

FASHIONING, IMITATIONS AND SYNTHETICS

Milky quartz is rarely cut as a gemstone and is most often cut into beads or ornaments. It may contain grains of gold and is usually cut en cabochon to show these.

SPECIFIC GRAVITY 2.65	HARDNESS 7.0		CRYSTAL SYSTEM **TRIGONAL**		DOUBLY REFRACTIVE **1.54–1.55**	BIREFRINGENCE **0.009**

QUARTZ CAT'S-EYE

QUARTZ GROUP
CHEMICAL COMPOSITION: SILICA

PHYSICAL AND OPTICAL PROPERTIES

Quartz cat's-eye is one of a group formed from fibrous quartz aggregates. It is semi-transparent and the fibres are clearly seen. Another variety, tiger's-eye, varies in colour from gold-yellow to gold-brown stripes against a blackish background. Hawk's-eye is blue. Quartz cat's-eye contains parallel lines of asbestos fibres. It becomes greenish grey or green when ground. Tiger's-eyes and hawk's-eyes form when blue crocidolite asbestos is replaced by quartz. The asbestos breaks down leaving a residue of brown iron oxides, which gives the golden brown colours in tiger's-eye. Hawk's-eye retains the original blue colour of asbestos.

LOCALITIES AND ROCK TYPES

Quartz cat's-eye is found in Burma, India, Sri Lanka and Germany. Tiger's-eye and hawk's-eye are mainly found in South Africa, but other localities include Australia, Burma, India and the USA.

FASHIONING, IMITATIONS AND SYNTHETICS

Tiger's-eye is often used for carving boxes and other ornamental items. It can also be cut to show the chatoyant (cat's-eye) effect. Quartz cat's-eye is usually cut into round polished pieces for jewellery.

Quartz cat's-eye may be distinguished from chrysoberyl cat's-eye by its refractive index.

| SPECIFIC GRAVITY 2.65 | HARDNESS 7.0 | CRYSTAL SYSTEM **TRIGONAL** | DOUBLY REFRACTIVE **1.54–1.55** | BIREFRINGENCE **0.009** |

AVENTURINE QUARTZ

QUARTZ GROUP
CHEMICAL COMPOSITION: SILICA

PHYSICAL AND OPTICAL PROPERTIES

Aventurine quartz is named after a type of glass discovered in Italy at the beginning of the 18th century. It was called *a ventura* because the glass was discovered "by accident" or "luck". Aventurine quartz contains mica plates which give it a sheen, with spangles of different colours. Green aventurine quartz contains green mica. Other aventurine quartzes include the brownish-red stones, which contain cubes of the mineral pyrite. Other varieties of aventurine include bluish-white and bluish-green material.

LOCALITIES AND ROCK TYPES

The main localities for good quality aventurine include Brazil, India, Siberia and Tanzania.

FASHIONING, IMITATIONS AND SYNTHETICS

Aventurine is used for ornamental objects and may also be cut en cabochon.

| SPECIFIC GRAVITY 2.65 | HARDNESS 7.0 | CRYSTAL SYSTEM **TRIGONAL** | DOUBLY REFRACTIVE **1.54–1.55** | BIREFRINGENCE **0.009** |

CHALCEDONY

QUARTZ GROUP
CHEMICAL COMPOSITION: SILICA

PHYSICAL AND OPTICAL PROPERTIES

Chalcedony is a variety of quartz with a crystalline structure that is so small it can only be seen with the use of a microscope (microcrystalline). The word chalcedony covers a group of quartzes, including all agates, carnelian and chrysoprase, which form from thin layers of tiny quartz fibres. Pure chalcedony, however, has its own distinct properties. Chalcedony itself is translucent and has a white or bluish colour, but it may be coloured green by chromium. The banding of chalcedony cannot be seen without a microscope. Under ultraviolet light the luminescence of chalcedony varies from bluish-white to yellowish-green.

LOCALITIES AND ROCK TYPES

Good quality chalcedony is found in Brazil, India, Madagascar and Uruguay.

FASHIONING, IMITATIONS AND SYNTHETICS

The fibrous structure gives chalcedony its toughness and makes it ideal for carving, particularly popular in Germany. Chalcedony is porous and may be dyed with a variety of metallic salts.

SPECIFIC GRAVITY 2.60	HARDNESS 7.0	CRYSTAL SYSTEM **TRIGONAL**	DOUBLY REFRACTIVE **1.54 (mean)**	BIREFRINGENCE **rarely seen**

JASPER

QUARTZ GROUP
CHEMICAL COMPOSITION: SILICA

PHYSICAL AND OPTICAL PROPERTIES

Jasper is an impure variety of microcrystalline quartz. It consists of a network of interlocking quartz crystals. The word jasper comes from the Greek word meaning "spotted stone". Jasper is opaque and may contain a mixture of reds and browns or greyish-blues and greens, caused by impurities such as red and yellow iron oxides or green chlorite and actinolite. Riband (ribbon) jasper is striped. A red and green ribbon jasper, found in Russia, takes a good polish but may break along lines where the colours meet. Orbicular jasper has white or grey "eyes" surrounded by red jasper. Bloodstone or heliotrope is a dark green opaque variety of jasper with scattered red spots. Plasma is also opaque and is usually green with white or yellow spots. Hornstone is a grey impure form which is sometimes stained blue to imitate lapis lazuli. Prase is a dull green rock sometimes coloured by actinolite fibres.

LOCALITIES AND ROCK TYPES

Jasper is found worldwide. A red jasper is found in India and Venezuela, but the most varied types are found in the USA, in particular in Santa Clara, California, where orbicular jasper is found.

FASHIONING, IMITATIONS AND SYNTHETICS

Jasper is often cut in slabs for fireplace surrounds, tables and facing materials. It is also used for carvings and in mosaics and inlays. Jasper may form within fossil wood and when polished this petrified wood is attractive in brooches or cut en cabochon.

SPECIFIC GRAVITY 2.60	HARDNESS 7.0	CRYSTAL SYSTEM **TRIGONAL**	DOUBLY REFRACTIVE **1.54 (mean)**	BIREFRINGENCE **rarely seen**

AGATES

QUARTZ GROUP
CHEMICAL COMPOSITION: SILICA

PHYSICAL AND OPTICAL PROPERTIES
Agates are banded forms of chalcedony. The bands may be multicoloured or different shades of the same colour. Coloration is due to different quantities of trace elements and the banding is due to the progressive solidification of the material. When agate contains dendritic (tree-like) inclusions it is called moss agate or mocha stone. The inclusions may be black (manganese dioxide), green (chlorite), red (iron) or a mixture. Fire agate has iridescent colours which are produced by the interference of light at the layers of iron oxide within the chalcedony.

LOCALITIES AND ROCK TYPES
Agate localities include Brazil, Egypt, Scotland and Uruguay. The best green moss agate comes from India.

FASHIONING, IMITATIONS AND SYNTHETICS
Agate is usually cut and polished and may be stained many different colours. Agate can chip and splinter when struck.

SPECIFIC GRAVITY 2.60 HARDNESS 7.0

 CRYSTAL SYSTEM **TRIGONAL**

 DOUBLY REFRACTIVE **1.54 (mean)**

BIREFRINGENCE **rarely seen**

SARD, SARDONYX AND ONYX

QUARTZ GROUP
CHEMICAL COMPOSITION: SILICA

PHYSICAL AND OPTICAL PROPERTIES
Sard is the brownish-red variety of chalcedony. Sardonyx has straight bands of white together with bands of brownish-red sard. Onyx is made up of black and white bands. It is similar to agate except that the bands are straight.

LOCALITIES AND ROCK TYPES
Localities include Brazil and Uruguay.

FASHIONING, IMITATIONS AND SYNTHETICS
Sard, sardonyx and onyx are carved and polished for use as beads and cameos.

Black onyx has almost always been stained. Natural black onyx is rare and so it is produced by chemically treating agate.

onyx   *sardonyx*

SPECIFIC GRAVITY 2.60 HARDNESS 7.0

 CRYSTAL SYSTEM **TRIGONAL**

 DOUBLY REFRACTIVE **1.54 (mean)**

BIREFRINGENCE **rarely seen**

CHRYSOPRASE

QUARTZ GROUP
CHEMICAL COMPOSITION: SILICA

PHYSICAL AND OPTICAL PROPERTIES
Chrysoprase is a form of chalcedony.
It is translucent and apple green.

LOCALITIES AND ROCK TYPES
Most early chrysoprase came from
Bohemia. A more recent source is
Marlborough in Queensland, Australia.

FASHIONING, IMITATIONS AND SYNTHETICS
It is usually cut en cabochon, as beads,

which are thought to date from Greek
and Roman times. Like other rare
gemstones, chrysoprase is imitated.
These imitations include glass and
stained agate.

| SPECIFIC GRAVITY 2.60 | HARDNESS 7.0 | | CRYSTAL SYSTEM **TRIGONAL** | DOUBLY REFRACTIVE **1.54 (mean)** | BIREFRINGENCE **rarely seen** |

CARNELIAN

QUARTZ GROUP
CHEMICAL COMPOSITION: SILICA

PHYSICAL AND OPTICAL PROPERTIES
Carnelian, also known as cornelian, is
the translucent red variety of chalcedony.
The red colour comes from the presence
of iron oxides.

LOCALITIES AND ROCK TYPES
Carnelian is found as rolled pebbles in
Brazil, China, Egypt and India. Other
localities include Colombia, Germany,
Japan, Scotland and the USA.

FASHIONING, IMITATIONS AND SYNTHETICS
Carnelian is carved or cut and polished
en cabochon.
Most commercial carnelian is stained
chalcedony.

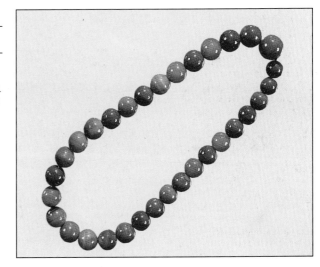

| SPECIFIC GRAVITY 2.60 | HARDNESS 7.0 | | CRYSTAL SYSTEM **TRIGONAL** | DOUBLY REFRACTIVE **1.54 (mean)** | BIREFRINGENCE **rarely seen** |

– THE PLAY OF COLOUR IN OPAL –

The flashes of colour seen in precious opal are called the play of colour. For hundreds of years theories have been put forward to explain the reasons for this phenomenon, but it is only recently that laboratory equipment has been sufficiently advanced to give the true story. Baier in Germany and Sanders in Australia both examined the structure of opal using an electron microscope which is able to magnify the structure more than 1000 times. They saw that areas of precious opal were made up of regularly arranged rows of silica spheres of similar size. Where the spheres are not similar there is no play of colour and the opal is referred to as common opal, milky opal or "potch".

The play of colour is due to diffraction of light by the spheres. The colours seen depend on the size of the spheres. Larger spheres give red, yellow, green, blue and white, while smaller spheres may give only blue flashes of colour.

OPAL

QUARTZ GROUP
CHEMICAL COMPOSITION: SILICA AND WATER

There are four types of opal commonly used in jewellery: white, black, fire and water opal. Opals are also classified as either common or precious stones; only the precious stones display iridescence. The name opal is thought to come from the Sanskrit word for precious stone – *upala*.

PHYSICAL AND OPTICAL PROPERTIES
Opal is one of the few non-crystalline, or poorly-crystalline, gemstones. It is a hardened jelly made up of silica and water. It is found filling cavities in rocks, as stalagmites or replacing organic matter such as shell and bone. It has an uneven or conchoidal fracture. White opal has a light-coloured body colour with a good play of colour, showing all the spectral colours. Black opal has a dark body colour (black, blue, green or grey) and a good play of colour. Fire opal is a transparent yellow, orange or red stone which may show a play of colour. Water opal is a clear and colourless stone with flashes of colour. The play of colour, or iridescence, is due to the interference of white light on minute silica spheres in the structure of opal (see the box opposite).

LOCALITIES AND ROCK TYPES
Opal used by the Romans came from Czechoslovakia where white opal was found in volcanic lava and mined from tunnels dug deep into the mountains. Guatemala, Honduras and Mexico are opal localities, but since the discovery of precious opal in Queensland, Australia, they have become less important. The first type of opal to be found in Australia was boulder opal, used in cameo carving. Opal also occurs in sedimentary and igneous rocks in veins, as lumps or in pipes and may replace organic matter forming opalized fossils of shellfish or dinosaur bones, such as those found at White Cliffs, New South Wales. At Lightning Ridge in New South Wales, isolated nodules of black opal are found. Precious white opal is found at Coober Pedy in South Australia. Other localities include Brazil, South Africa, Zimbabwe and the USA.

FASHIONING, IMITATIONS AND SYNTHETICS
Fire opals are usually faceted, but other opals are cut en cabochon or carved. Opal has been imitated in several ways; one method is to place chips of coloured plastic and opal behind a hollow-backed cabochon of rock crystal. Another is to cement iridescent shell to the back of a flat-based cabochon of rock crystal. Gilson has manufactured "Created" opals from silica spheres.

SPECIFIC GRAVITY 2.10   **HARDNESS** 6.0    CRYSTAL SYSTEM **AMORPHOUS**   SINGLY REFRACTIVE **1.45**

PYROPE

GARNET GROUP

CHEMICAL COMPOSITION: MAGNESIUM ALUMINIUM SILICATE

PHYSICAL AND OPTICAL PROPERTIES

Pyrope is usually red. It is coloured by iron and sometimes also by chromium. Pyrope does not fluoresce under ultraviolet light due to its iron content, but red spinel, which is similar, does. Pyrope is moderately magnetic and this can also be used to separate it from red spinel. The pyrope absorption spectrum is characterized by three dark bands. The bright red stones from Czechoslavkia, Arizona (USA) and Kimberley (South Africa) have a typical chromium spectrum with a narrow doublet in the red and a broad band. Pyrope rarely has inclusions. When they are present they are usually small rounded crystals with irregular outlines.

LOCALITIES AND ROCK TYPES

Pyrope from Czechoslovakia is found in conglomerates, volcanic rocks and in various alluvials, but rarely as good crystals. Most pyrope now used is found in the diamond mines of South Africa.

Russian pyrope is also of good quality. Other localities include Argentina, Australia , Brazil, Burma and Tanzania.

FASHIONING, IMITATIONS AND SYNTHETICS

Most pyrope is faceted for setting in jewellery and was particularly popular in the nineteenth century.

SPECIFIC GRAVITY 3.70–3.90 **HARDNESS** 7–7.5

 CRYSTAL SYSTEM **ISOMETRIC**

 SINGLY REFRACTIVE **1.73–1.76**

ALMANDINE

GARNET GROUP

CHEMICAL COMPOSITION: IRON ALUMINIUM SILICATE

PHYSICAL AND OPTICAL PROPERTIES

Red almandine and pyrope are the most widely used of all garnets. Almandine is usually a darker red than the blood-red of pyrope. Cut crystals have a brilliant lustre, but their transparency is sometimes marred by excessive depth of colour. Inclusions such as "zircon haloes" and orientated needle-shaped or rod-like crystals of minerals such as hornblende (which give the stones a silky lustre) are seen in Sri Lankan almandine garnets.

LOCALITIES AND ROCK TYPES

Almandine is found worldwide in metamorphic rocks such as garnet mica schists. India is a good source of gem-quality almandine. Other localities include Central and South America (in particular Brazil), Madagascar, Tanzania and Zambia. There are many deposits in Brazil and gem-quality almandine has been found in Austria. Scottish almandine is opaque and too dark to facet.

FASHIONING, IMITATIONS AND SYNTHETICS

Almandine is usually faceted in the mixed-cut style or occasionally the trap-cut style. Star stones, and those too dark to facet, are cut en cabochon. Irregular-shaped pieces may be fashioned by tumbling to be used as beads. Almandine cabochons are called "carbuncles".

SPECIFIC GRAVITY 3.90–4.20 **HARDNESS** 7.5

 CRYSTAL SYSTEM **ISOMETRIC**

 SINGLY REFRACTIVE **1.76–1.81**

– CHARACTERISTICS OF GARNET –

Garnet is the name of a group of silicates with various amounts of magnesium, iron or calcium. The garnets can be divided into two series, the pyrope-almandine series ("pyralspite" series) and the uvarovite-grossularite-andradite series ("ugrandite" series). Within each series there is a continuous change in physical and optical characteristics from one end to the other.

Crystals are found as rhombic dodecahedra (12-faced) and icositetrahedra (24-faced) and combinations of these. They show no cleavage and fracture is subconchoidal to uneven.

SPESSARTINE

GARNET GROUP
CHEMICAL COMPOSITION: MANGANESE ALUMINIUM SILICATE

PHYSICAL AND OPTICAL PROPERTIES
The name is derived from the Spessart district of Germany, where the crystals were once found. Petrologists, who study the origin and structure of rocks, refer to the rock itself as spessartite, but the gems are referred to as spessartine. Spessartine garnets are orange-pink, orange-red, red-brown or brownish yellow in colour. They have a characteristic absorption spectrum which is partly due to the presence of manganese. Spessartine is inert under ultraviolet light and X-rays. There are characteristic lace- or feather-like inclusions which can only be detected by experts. Hessonite garnet is similar in colour but has quite different inclusions which give it a treacly appearance.

LOCALITIES AND ROCK TYPES
Gem-quality examples are rare. Most of the crystals found in Germany and Italy are too small to be used in jewellery, but good examples are found in Australia (New South Wales), Burma, Madagascar, Norway and the USA (Virginia and California). Some gem-quality spessartine is found in Brazil, but the majority is too dark to be of use in jewellery.

FASHIONING, IMITATIONS AND SYNTHETICS
Spessartine may be faceted or cut en cabochon.

SPECIFIC GRAVITY 4.16	**HARDNESS** 7.0	

CRYSTAL SYSTEM
ISOMETRIC

SINGLY REFRACTIVE
1.80

GROSSULAR GARNET

GARNET GROUP
CHEMICAL COMPOSITION: CALCIUM ALUMINIUM SILICATE

PHYSICAL AND OPTICAL PROPERTIES
The name grossular is derived from the Latin for gooseberries. Grossular garnets are usually opaque and have little use in jewellery, but there are some varieties which are transparent or semi-opaque and may be cut as gemstones.

Hessonite garnets are a yellowish-brown to orange-red variety which have characteristic inclusions that look like swirls, giving a treacle-like appearance. Pure grossular is colourless. "Transvaal jade", a massive grossular garnet from South Africa, is also green or grey, blue or pink.

LOCALITIES AND ROCK TYPES
Hessonite is found in the gem gravels of Sri Lanka and in Brazil, Canada, Russia and the USA. Green grossular garnet has been found in Tanzania and more recently in Kenya, and has been called "Tsavorite".

FASHIONING, IMITATIONS AND SYNTHETICS
Grossular garnets may be faceted or cut en cabochon. "Transvaal jade", which contains specks of magnetite, makes an attractive stone when carved.

SPECIFIC GRAVITY 3.65	**HARDNESS** 7–7.5	CRYSTAL SYSTEM **ISOMETRIC**	SINGLY REFRACTIVE **1.74**

ANDRADITE

GARNET GROUP
CHEMICAL COMPOSITION: CALCIUM IRON SILICATE

PHYSICAL AND OPTICAL PROPERTIES
Andradite garnet has two varieties that have been used in jewellery. One is opaque black melanite, which has been used for mourning jewellery. The other is green demantoid garnet, the colour of which is due to the presence of chromium. Melanite crystals are usually dodecahedra or icositetrahedra or a mixture of both.

Demantoid is a rare variety of andradite. It has a higher dispersion than diamond, but the vivid green colour masks this property. It is relatively soft and so is not commonly used in jewellery. Demantoid garnet looks red through the Chelsea colour filter and has a characteristic absorption spectrum with a strong band in the red which is due to iron. It is inert under ultraviolet light and X-rays. Inclusions are groups of radiating asbestos fibres which look like "horse-tails". Demantoid is the only green mineral that has these horse-tails.

LOCALITIES AND ROCK TYPES
The main source for gem-quality demantoid is the Ural Mountains. It is also found in Zaire and Korea, although these are not of such good quality. Melanite is found in Italy and the Haute-Pyrenees of France. Topazolite is the name given to yellow andradite garnet.

FASHIONING, IMITATIONS AND SYNTHETICS
Andradite garnet is faceted for use in jewellery.

SPECIFIC GRAVITY 3.85	**HARDNESS** 6.5	CRYSTAL SYSTEM **ISOMETRIC**	SINGLY REFRACTIVE **1.89**

TOURMALINE

CHEMICAL COMPOSITION: COMPLEX BOROSILICATE

There are a greater number of colours of tourmaline than of any other gemstone. They include red and pink (rubellite), blue (indicolite), colourless (achroite), brown (dravite), violet (siberite), yellow, green and black (schorl). Tourmaline may also be parti-coloured, showing two colours in the one stone. A type with a pink centre and green surround is referred to as "water-melon" tourmaline. A single crystal may also show a different colour at either end of the crystal, for instance pink and green.

PHYSICAL AND OPTICAL PROPERTIES

The crystals are usually long thin prisms that are vertically striated. They show a characteristic rounded triangular section when viewed down their length. The terminations at either end of a crystal are differently shaped. Tourmaline has an uneven fracture and no cleavage. Lustre is vitreous and transparency varies from transparent to opaque. The refractive indices are different for each colour. Birefringence is high and a doubling of the back facets should be apparent in cut stones. Dichroism is more obvious in the darker stones with two shades of the body colour visible in the principal optical directions. The absorption spectrum is usually too weak to be used for identification and luminescence is not distinctive. Inclusions are black patches or thread-like fluid-filled cavities which may sometimes be cut en cabochon to show a cat's-eye.

When tourmaline, apart from the black and dark coloured iron-rich varieties, is heated it becomes electrically charged. One end of the crystal becomes positively charged and the other negatively charged and the crystal may attract small pieces of paper or dust

towards one end. Because dust is attracted, tourmaline in a jeweller's window display will appear dusty sooner than most other gemstones. When pressure is applied to tourmaline it also becomes charged; this property is used in some depth-recording equipment.

LOCALITIES AND ROCK TYPES

Tourmaline is found in schists and pegmatic rocks. Crystals may be found in cavities within rock or weathered out and found in alluvial deposits or as water-worn pebbles in streams. The Ural Mountains of Russia have well-known gem-quality tourmaline localities. These are blue or red and are found in yellow clays formed from weathered granites. Much gem-quality tourmaline comes from pegmatic rocks in Madagascar. Red varieties are the most popular and colourless the most rare, but all colours are found there. Sri Lanka has yellow and brown coloured tourmalines which

are found in alluvial deposits. Fine red tourmaline is found in Burma. Tourmaline from Brazil is green, blue or red and many of the crystals are parti-coloured. Bright green tourmaline crystals coloured by chromium (and sometimes vanadium) have been found in Tanzania. Dark green tourmaline crystals from Namibia are usually lightened by heating. Other localities include South Africa, Zimbabwe, Mozambique, Kenya and the USA (California, Connecticut and Maine).

FASHIONING, IMITATIONS AND SYNTHETICS

The mixed cut (step-cut pavilion and brilliant-cut crown) and the trap cut are used for fashioning most tourmaline. Flawed tourmaline is used to make beads and may be carved as small figurines. When it is cut en cabochon it may show the cat's-eye effect. The black "schorl" tourmaline has been used for mourning jewellery.

| **SPECIFIC GRAVITY** 3.06 | **HARDNESS** 7.5 | CRYSTAL SYSTEM **TRIGONAL** | DOUBLY REFRACTIVE **1.62–1.64** | BIREFRINGENCE **0.018** |

39

TOPAZ

CHEMICAL COMPOSITION: ALUMINIUM FLUOROSILICATE WITH SOME HYDROXYL

Topaz is colourless, blue, green, sherry-yellow or port-red and, very rarely, pink. The name may have been derived from the Sanskrit word *tapas*, meaning fire.

Crystal, carving and heat treated blue topaz.

PHYSICAL AND OPTICAL PROPERTIES

Topaz is found as prismatic crystals deeply striated parallel to the length of the crystal. They are usually terminated at one end only, the shape of the termination depending upon locality. Topaz has basal cleavage. The crystals show a typical and distinctive lozenge shape when viewed down their length. The high birefringence causes a doubling of the back facets which can be seen through the front of a cut stone. Topaz has a vitreous lustre and a characteristic slippery feel.

There is distinct pleochroism showing no colour and a weak and a stronger shade of the body colour. It is particularly noticeable in pink, sherry-yellow and blue stones. Only the sherry-brown topazes have a noticeable absorption spectrum. Under long-wave ultraviolet light there may be slight luminescence, but this luminescence is weaker under short-wave ultraviolet light except for the sherry-brown and the pink topazes which show an orange luminescence. When gently heated or rubbed with a finger topazes become electrically charged. Inclusions are tear-shaped cavities which may contain several immiscible (non-mixing) liquids.

LOCALITIES AND ROCK TYPES

Topaz occurs in cavities within rocks such as granite or rhyolite and in pegmatite dykes. Much is found as water-worn pebbles in alluvial deposits. Sherry-brown topaz is found in the state of Minas Gerais, Brazil as detached crystals embedded in a clay and can be heat-treated to give attractive pink stones. Blue and white topaz crystals and rolled pebbles are also found in Brazil. Topaz with a slight blue colour is usually irradiated with gamma rays to darken its colour and make a more attractive stone. Colourless, pale blue, reddish and yellow crystals are found in the USA, particularly in the Pike's Peak region of Colorado. Blue, colourless and pale brown topaz from Tasmania and Queensland and New South Wales, Australia are found as rolled pebbles with few flaws or as crystals. Other localities include Russia, many of the countries of Africa, Sri Lanka, Burma and Japan. Non gem-quality topaz is found in Northern Ireland, the Cairngorm mountains of Scotland and St Michael's mount and Lundy Island off the Cornish and Devon coasts of England.

FASHIONING, IMITATIONS AND SYNTHETICS

Topaz is often cut as oval or pendeloque (drop-shaped) stones using the mixed-cut style. Dark coloured topaz may be cut in the trap-cut style. Pale pink topaz may be backed by red coloured foil in a closed setting to give the appearance of a stronger coloured stone.

Natural and synthetic corundum may have colours similar to topaz but these can be distinguished by their different refractive indices.

SPECIFIC GRAVITY 3.50–3.60 **HARDNESS** 8.0

CRYSTAL SYSTEM ORTHORHOMBIC	**DOUBLY REFRACTIVE** 1.62–1.64

BIREFRINGENCE 0.008–0.010

PERIDOT

CHEMICAL COMPOSITION: MAGNESIUM IRON SILICATE

Peridot is bottle green in colour. The colour is due to iron and peridot is said to be idiochromatic because iron is an essential constituent of peridot. Peridot is the name given to the mineral olivine by gemmologists. It used to be known as topaz (a name now used for a different gem species) after the locality of Topazios, an island in the Red Sea now called St John's Island.

PHYSICAL AND OPTICAL PROPERTIES

Crystals are found as vertically striated flattened prisms. A peridot weighing 319 carats may be seen at the Smithsonian Museum, Washington, USA and one of 136 carats at the Natural History Museum in London, England. Doubling of the back facets can be seen using a hand lens. There is little dispersion and lustre is vitreous and oily. Pleochroism is weak. Peridot has a distinctive absorption spectrum with three broad lines in the blue caused by the presence of iron.

Inclusions, which look like "water-lily leaves" are due to recrystallization of liquid inside cavities. Inclusions of mica flakes often have brown rims. Hawaiian peridot may have inclusions of tear-shaped glass drops that look like bubbles. A stone with a single inclusion appears to have two, because the high double refraction shows a doubling of the outline.

LOCALITIES AND ROCK TYPES

The most important source of peridot was St John's Island, but the island is no longer accessible for collecting. Gem-quality stones are found in the Mogok area of Burma. Crystals and rolled pebbles have been found in Norway, Australia and Brazil. Peridot from New Mexico and Arizona (USA) has been found in sands and even in ant-hills. Other localities include the diamondiferous "pipes" of South Africa. Pebbles are found on the beaches of Hawaii. Peridot has been found as far afield as Antarctica and it has even been found in meteorites.

FASHIONING, IMITATIONS AND SYNTHETICS

Peridot is usually cut in the trap-cut style. Oval, pendeloque, round and mixed cuts are also used. Because of its softness, peridot is fashioned into brooches, pendants and earrings but it is seldom used as a gemstone in rings or bracelets.

Glass and composite stones including garnet topped doublets and synthetic spinel composites (using green-coloured cement to join two pieces of spinel) are used to imitate peridot but these should be recognizeable by the fact that they lack the oily lustre.

SPECIFIC GRAVITY 3.34 **HARDNESS** 6.5–7.0 CRYSTAL SYSTEM **ORTHORHOMBIC** DOUBLY REFRACTIVE **1.64–1.69** BIREFRINGENCE **0.035**

ZIRCON

CHEMICAL COMPOSITION: ZIRCONIUM SILICATE

Colours range from colourless, yellow, red, orange, brown, yellowish-green, bright green, dark green to sky-blue. Colourless, golden-brown and sky-blue are most popular in jewellery and often have their colour enhanced by heat treatment. The name zircon is derived from the word *zargoon*, which means vermillion in Arabic and gold-coloured in Persian.

PHYSICAL AND OPTICAL PROPERTIES

The crystals are usually found as square prisms with pyramidal terminations. There is imperfect cleavage and fracture is conchoidal. There are no particularly characteristic inclusions within zircons although they may appear cloudy or have angular zoning and are occasionally chatoyant.

There are two types of zircons. "High type" zircon which is used in jewellery breaks down into "low type" zircon as a result of radioactive decay of elements within the zircon. Heat can change the low type back into the high type. Radioactive decay affects the physical and optical properties of the zircon, but zircon jewellery is no danger to the wearer.

Zircon has a high birefringence and doubling of the back facets can easily be seen, but dichroism is rarely apparent. Blue zircons which are heat treated, however, do show a strong dichroism (colourless and blue). Zircon has almost as much fire as diamond and is used as a diamond simulant. Zircon has a characteristic absorption spectrum which is due to uranium, with many strong absorption bands visible. Under ultraviolet light and X-rays, the stone's appearance varies from almost inert to a strong fluorescence.

LOCALITIES AND ROCK TYPES

Zircon is a common mineral and can be found in igneous rocks worldwide. Much gem-quality zircon is found in the gem gravels of Sri Lanka, in the Mogok area of Burma and in Thailand. The main zircon gem localities in Thailand are the Champasak, Pailin and Kha districts. Rough zircon from Kha is heat-treated to give blue, golden and colourless stones. Well-formed red crystals are found in France, brown crystals in Norway and near-white rolled pebbles have been found in Tanzania. Gem-quality zircon is also found in Australia.

FASHIONING, IMITATIONS AND SYNTHETICS

Zircon is faceted, usually as round brilliants. Although it is moderately hard, the facet edges of zircon are easily chipped when worn.

Synthetic blue spinel is used to imitate blue zircon and coloured glass is used to imitate other colours. Most vivid blue, golden or colourless zircons are heat-treated brown zircons .

SPECIFIC GRAVITY 4.5–4.7   **HARDNESS** 6.5–7.5

 CRYSTAL SYSTEM **TETRAGONAL**

 DOUBLY REFRACTIVE **1.92–2.02**   BIREFRINGENCE **0.059**

CHRYSOBERYL

CHEMICAL COMPOSITION: BERYLLIUM ALUMINIUM OXIDE

Chrysoberyls are green, greenish-yellow or brown in colour. There are two varieties of chrysoberyl, alexandrite, and the variety which shows the property of chatoyancy and is called the cat's-eye. The alexandrites are distinctive in that they show a colour change. In daylight they are green, but when viewed under artificial light they appear red. Some replacement of aluminium by chromium gives the green colour to alexandrite.

PHYSICAL AND OPTICAL PROPERTIES

Chrysoberyl is found as prismatic crystals which are usually flattened parallel to one pair of the faces Alexandrite may be found as three intergrown crystals which give the appearance of having hexagonal symmetry; these are called "trillings". There are three directions of cleavage which are weak, and fracture is conchoidal. Alexandrite shows a weak red glow under ultraviolet light and under X-rays. The cat's-eye effect shown by some chrysoberyl crystals is due to the reflection of light from inclusions which are like fine canals or needles within the stone.

LOCALITIES AND ROCK TYPES

The best alexandrites are found in mica schists in the Ural Mountains of Russia. Russian chrysoberyl has two-phase inclusions (a bubble within a liquid-filled cavity) and feathers. Larger crystals of chrysoberyl are found as water-worn pebbles in the gem gravels of Sri Lanka, but these are generally not of such a good quality as those from Russia. Other localities include the Mogok area of Burma, the states of Minas Gerais, Espirito Santos and Bahia in Brazil, and Zimbabwe, Madagascar, Zambia and Tanzania.

FASHIONING, IMITATIONS AND SYNTHETICS

The mixed cut (brilliant-cut crown and trap-cut pavilion) is usually used for chrysoberyl. To show the cat's-eye the stone must be cut en cabochon. Chrysoberyl cat's-eyes, not to be confused with quartz cat's-eyes, are greenish yellow or yellow, often with a cold, greyish tone. They contain a moving green light ray which, with the colour, gives them their name. Synthetic chrysoberyl, synthetic corundum and synthetic spinel are made to imitate alexandrite and its colour change.

SPECIFIC GRAVITY 3.68–3.78 **HARDNESS** 8.5

 CRYSTAL SYSTEM **ORTHORHOMBIC** DOUBLY REFRACTIVE **1.74–1.76** BIREFRINGENCE **0.009**

SPINEL

CHEMICAL COMPOSITION: MAGNESIUM ALUMINIUM OXIDE

Spinels are found in a number of different colours including shades of red, blue, violet, purple and mauve. Dark green and brown iron-rich spinels are usually too dark to be used in jewellery. Black spinels have been found on the volcano Vesuvius in Italy. Star stones are also found occasionally. Iron-rich spinels are termed *ceylonites* and zinc-rich spinels are termed *gahnospinels*. The name spinel is probably derived from the Latin *spina*, meaning a thorn. Red spinel has been known as "Balas ruby" after a place in northern India where the stones were thought to be found. The "Black Prince's Ruby" (uncut) set in the front of the Imperial State Crown and the "Timur Ruby" (engraved) are both in the British crown jewels and are both spinels.

PHYSICAL AND OPTICAL PROPERTIES

Spinel is found as octahedral crystals which may be twinned and as perfect crystals such as those from the Mogok area of Burma. Spinel is also found as pebbles in gem gravels

Spinels have a vitreous lustre and take a good polish. Red spinels show a characteristic absorption spectrum, with a group of fine lines in the red which have been called "organ-pipe" fluorescent lines. Synthetic spinel coloured with cobalt is used to imitate blue spinel but these can easily be distinguished by their different absorption spectra. A weak red glow is seen when a red spinel is placed under short-wave ultraviolet light, while a much stronger and brighter glow is seen under long-wave ultraviolet light. Spinel rarely has inclusions. When present, they are in the form of large angular inclusions which cause the appearance of iridescent spots called "spangles"

Inclusions of solid crystals such as magnelite may be present.

LOCALITIES AND ROCK TYPES

Spinel is generally found in association with corundum, usually in alluvial deposits such as those of Burma and Sri Lanka. Other localities include Afghanistan, Thailand, Australia, Sweden, Brazil and the USA.

FASHIONING, IMITATIONS AND SYNTHETICS

Spinels are fashioned in the mixed-cut or trap-cut styles although in the past octahedral crystals were sometimes set in jewellery without any faceting. The star stones when cut en cabochon show a four-rayed star.

Spinel is made synthetically. It is coloured to imitate other gemstones such as aquamarine and zircon.

SPECIFIC GRAVITY 3.60–3.70 **HARDNESS** 8.0

 CRYSTAL SYSTEM **ISOMETRIC**

 SINGLY REFRACTIVE **1.71–1.75**

T U R Q U O I S E

CHEMICAL COMPOSITION: **HYDRATED PHOSPHATE OF COPPER AND ALUMINIUM**

Turquoise mining has been carried out in or near Egypt since 3000BC. The name is derived from the French *pierre turquoise* (*tourques* in old French) possibly because the Persian (Iranian) material was imported to Europe via Turkey.

PHYSICAL AND OPTICAL PROPERTIES

Turquoise forms as a porous blue cryptocrystalline aggregate and is found as encrustations, nodules or botryoidal masses or in veins within rocks in arid regions. It has been found as distinct crystals but only in Virginia, USA. The blue colour is due to copper and/or iron. It may fade with excess sunlight and alter to a green colour, possibly due to dehydration. American turquoise is more porous than Iranian turquoise and fades and alters more rapidly.

Turquoise is semi-translucent, and the absorption spectrum has a characteristic pattern of weak bands. Under long-wave ultraviolet light turquoise appears a greenish-yellow to bright blue. It is inert under short-wave ultraviolet light, whereas some imitations of turquoise show a strong blue colour. Gilson "Created" turquoise appears a dull blue under both long- and short-wave ultraviolet light.

LOCALITIES AND ROCK TYPES

The best turquoise is the sky-blue turquoise from Iran. In Tibet it is the green turquoise that is more highly prized. The Sinai peninsula of Egypt is the most historically important source and is the source of many of the early pieces. The ancient Aztecs and Incas used turquoise for ornaments and artifacts which came from mines in New Mexico. Other localities in the USA

include the Mohave (Mojave) desert, Colorado, which has quality compact turquoise of a good colour, and Nevada and Arizona. The turquoise from the USA is lighter in colour and more porous and chalky than that of Iran and Mexico. Other localities include Russia, Cornwall in England, Chile and Australia (Victoria and Queensland).

FASHIONING, IMITATIONS AND SYNTHETICS

Turquoise has a wax-like lustre and takes a good polish. It is carved, cut en cabochon or cut flat for inlay work. It may be engraved and inlaid with gold. Natural minerals which resemble turquoise include lazulite, wardite and odontolite (blue-coloured fossil tooth or

bone). Stained howlite, stained limestone and marble are also used as imitations. Turquoise was one of the earliest gems to be imitated. Imitations have been made from glass, which can usually be distinguished by inclusions of small bubbles or pit marks on the surface, and also from enamel or stained chalcedony. In the USA small pieces of friable turquoise are bonded by resin to make them usable in jewellery, but some fade or turn green with \time. A Gilson "Created" turquoise was manufactured in 1972 in France. Microscopic examination shows that the structure is made of blue angular pieces on a white background, which is quite different from turquoise.

JADEITE

CHEMICAL COMPOSITION: SODIUM ALUMINIUM SILICATE

Jadeite is the rarer "jade". It is found in a large variety of colours, but it is the dark emerald green ("imperial green") that is the most prized in jewellery. White, pink, brown, red, orange, yellow, mauve (due to manganese), blue, violet, black, shades of green and mottled green and white jadeites also occur. The presence of iron tends to give a dull green jadeite.

PHYSICAL AND OPTICAL PROPERTIES

Jadeite is found as a mass of interlocking granular crystals. This causes a dimpled effect when polished. It is less tough than nephrite jade. Jadeite has a characteristic absorption spectrum with a strong band in the blue and a pattern of weaker bands. The white, mauve, yellow and pale green stones show a whitish glow under long-wave ultraviolet light and a strong violet-coloured glow under X-rays, while the darker jadeite is inert. Green jadeite shows green under the Chelsea colour filter.

LOCALITIES AND ROCK TYPES

Burma is the most important source of jadeite. Burmese jadeite is found in metamorphic rocks and also as alluvial boulders. The boulders have a brown skin which is due to weathering. Boulders found in California (USA) since the 1930s are white, pale green, dark green and bluish-green, but they are semi-opaque and not of such good quality as the Burmese material. Green jadeite is found in Japan, but it is not of gem quality.

FASHIONING, IMITATIONS AND SYNTHETICS

Jadeite is used mainly for carvings. Small pieces may be used to make beads, cabochons, ring stones, brooches and drop earrings. The boulder material with a brown skin can be used to make cameos or snuff bottles which show both the skin and the internal colour in a single piece.

Jadeite has been imitated by bowenite which is a variety of serpentine. Bowenite is softer than jadeite and can be distinguished by the fact that it can easily be scratched with a knife. Jadeite has also been imitated by prehnite, feldspar, aventurine quartz, chrysoprase, stained serpentine, and green-coloured lead glass. "Transvaal jade" is a massive green grossular garnet which can be recognized by its orange fluorescence under x-rays and its higher density than jadeite.

SPECIFIC GRAVITY 3.30–3.50 **HARDNESS** 6.5–7.0

 CRYSTAL SYSTEM **MONOCLINIC**

 SINGLY REFRACTIVE **1.66** (mean)

N E P H R I T E

CHEMICAL COMPOSITION: CALCIUM MAGNESIUM IRON SILICATE

Nephrite is made up of an aggregate of fibrous (rather than granular) crystals which form a very tough interlocking structure. Colour ranges from a creamy colour ("mutton fat" jade) to dark green and depends on the chemical composition; the greater the iron content and smaller the magnesium content the darker the stone.

PHYSICAL AND OPTICAL PROPERTIES

Nephrite has a distinct absorption spectrum with a doublet in the red and a sharp line in the green. It shows no luminescence under ultraviolet light and looks green through the Chelsea colour filter.

LOCALITIES AND ROCK TYPES

Nephrite is found in eastern Turkestan. Most of the early Chinese jade carvings are of nephrite which was probably imported from Central Asia. It was not until the eighteenth century that jadeite from Burma was introduced.

Siberian nephrite is found as dark green boulders which may have black spots. New Zealand nephrite is found in talc-serpentine rocks on South Island and also on the D'Urville island between North and South Island. The dark green nephrite is found as pebbles in glacial deposits and used by Maoris to fashion ornaments and flattened clubs called meres. Considerable amounts of black nephrite are produced in South Australia. European localities include northern Italy, the Harz mountains of Germany and also Poland where nephrite is a

creamy white to sand colour with green patches. In Switzerland nephrite deposits were used by early lake dwellers. American nephrite is found in several states, including California, in a variety of colours mainly as alluvial deposits. Large boulders of yellow green to dark green nephrite have been found in Canada. Nephrite has also been found in Brazil and Taiwan and some good quality dark green nephrite has been found in Zimbabwe.

FASHIONING, IMITATIONS AND SYNTHETICS

Nephrite is mainly carved, although some Alaskan nephrite and some from the Rocky Mountains of the USA can be cut en cabochon to show the cat's-eye effect.

SPECIFIC GRAVITY 2.90–3.10 **HARDNESS** 6.5

 CRYSTAL SYSTEM **MONOCLINIC**

 SINGLY REFRACTIVE **1.62 (mean)**

LAPIS LAZULI

CHEMICAL COMPOSITION: LAZURITE (LAZURITE IS A MIXTURE OF SODALITE AND HAUYNITE), WITH SOME CALCITE AND PYRITE

The colour of lapis lazuli varies from a greenish-blue to a rich purple blue. A dark intense blue is the most prized colour. The rock was powdered and used for the pigment ultramarine, but since 1828 the pigment has been made synthetically. The name lapis lazuli is derived from the Persian word *lazhward*, meaning blue.

PHYSICAL AND OPTICAL PROPERTIES

Under long-wave ultraviolet light orange spots or streaks can be seen. These are more pronounced in the material from Chile than that from Afghanistan. Lapis lazuli shows a bright whitish glow under long-wave ultraviolet light and dull orange spots or streaks under short-wave ultraviolet and X-rays.

LOCALITIES AND ROCK TYPES

Afghanistan is the most famous locality of lapis lazuli which has been mined there for over 6000 years. The mines were described by Marco Polo in 1271. The lapis is found in black and white limestone high up in the mountains. Light blue boulders of lapis lazuli are found in rivers on the southern end of Lake Baikal, Russia. A paler coloured lapis lazuli is mined in the Chilean Andes. A very dark lapis lazuli was found in the Colorado Rockies in rocks formed by contact metamorphism; it contains pyrite but lacks the textures and hardness of good lapis. Other localities include California, Burma, Angola, Pakistan and Canada. Canadian lapis lazuli is blue-grey with patches of bright blue and white and contains pyrite, but is of little use as a gem material because of its porosity and because it does not take a good polish.

FASHIONING, IMITATIONS AND SYNTHETICS

Lapis lazuli is an opaque mineral and is therefore usually cut en cabochon or used as seal stones, beads, and small carved objects. It is also used as an inlay material.

Lapis lazuli has been imitated by blue-stained jasper ("Swiss lapis"), which can be recognized by its lack of pyrite inclusions. An imitation is also made using glass with copper inclusions. A synthetic spinel coloured blue by cobalt has been used in Germany to imitate lapis lazuli. Crushed lapis lazuli with included pyrite is bonded with plastic and some is dyed, but these are easily recognizable as a small amount of nail-varnish will remove the dye. Imitations can be recognized by their lack of a whitish glow under short-wave ultraviolet light.

Because lapis lazuli is a rock made up of a number of different minerals, it has been difficult to produce a true synthetic, but a Gilson "Created" lapis lazuli was produced in the mid 1970s. Although the colour is similar, the density is lower and the porosity higher than true lapis lazuli. The pyrite inclusions appear far too regularly arranged.

SPECIFIC GRAVITY 2.70–2.90 HARDNESS 5.5

 CRYSTAL SYSTEM **ISOMETRIC**

 SINGLY REFRACTIVE **1.50**

ORTHOCLASE

ALKALI FELDSPAR GROUP
CHEMICAL COMPOSITION: POTASSIUM ALUMINIUM SILICATE

PHYSICAL AND OPTICAL PROPERTIES

In its purest form, orthoclase is transparent and colourless and is a collector's gemstone. There are two directions of easy cleavage, at about 90° to each other (i.e. the directions are orthogonal, hence the name). Yellow orthoclase owes its colour to iron.

LOCALITIES AND ROCK TYPES

Orthoclase commonly occurs in intrusive, magmatic and metamorphic rocks where it has cooled slowly. The best examples of yellow orthoclase are found in Madagascar, where the cat's-eye variety is also found, and Germany.

Other varieties are distributed widely around the world, including western Europe and the USA.

FASHIONING, IMITATIONS AND SYNTHETICS

Yellow orthoclase is usually faceted as step-cut stones. It shows a cat's-eye effect when cut en cabochon. Colourless and pinkish-brown stones have also been cut.

SPECIFIC GRAVITY 2.56	**HARDNESS** 6.0–6.5	CRYSTAL SYSTEM **MONOCLINIC**	DOUBLY REFRACTIVE **1.53**	**BIREFRINGENCE** **0.005**

MOONSTONE

ALKALI FELDSPAR GROUP
CHEMICAL COMPOSITION: SODIUM POTASSIUM ALUMINIUM SILICATE

PHYSICAL AND OPTICAL PROPERTIES

Moonstone is a variety of orthoclase which has a blue schiller caused by the reflection of light from the internal structure of alternate layers of albite and orthoclase feldspar. Thicker layers give a white schiller rather than the most attractive blue schiller. There is no characteristic absorption spectrum. Luminescence is usually bluish under long-wave ultraviolet light and a weak orange under short-wave ultraviolet light, with a whitish to violet glow under X-rays (this may help to distinguish moonstone from its imitations).

LOCALITIES AND ROCK TYPES

Each locality may have characteristic inclusions. Sri Lankan moonstone usually has straight lath-like "stress cracks" which run parallel to the vertical axis of the crystal and from which there are branching cracks which appear to taper off. They may look like centipedes or other insects. Sri Lankan moonstone with a white or blue "flash" is found in

dykes or in water-worn pebbles in the gem gravels. Indian moonstone is characterized by the variations in body colour from white to reddish-brown or plum-blue and even green. Other localities include Madagascar, Burma, Tanzania and the USA (Colorado, Indiana, New Mexico, North Carolina, Pennsylvania, Virginia and Wisconsin).

FASHIONING, IMITATIONS AND SYNTHETICS

To show the sheen of moonstone to its best advantage, the stone should be cut en cabochon with the base of the cabochon parallel to the plane of the layers.

Heat is used to give synthetic white spinels a schiller to imitate moonstone. White chalcedony may also be cut en cabochon to imitate moonstone and may show a blue moon effect.

SPECIFIC GRAVITY 2.57	**HARDNESS** 6.0–6.5	CRYSTAL SYSTEM **MONOCLINIC**	DOUBLY REFRACTIVE **1.53**	**BIREFRINGENCE** **0.005**

AMAZONITE

ALKALI FELDSPAR
GROUP
CHEMICAL COMPOSITION: POTASSIUM ALUMINIUM
SILICATE

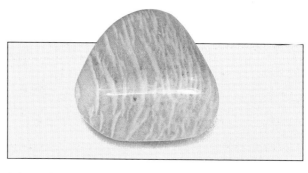

PHYSICAL AND OPTICAL PROPERTIES

The name amazonite is derived from the Amazon River. However, although there are localities in Brazil, there are none along this river. Amazonite is a type of microcline used as a gemstone. It is bright green to blue-green due to traces of lead and water. It has two directions of easy cleavage. The reflection from incipient cleavage cracks gives the polished surface a characteristic shimmering effect. There is no distinctive absorption spectrum. Under long-wave ultraviolet light amazonite looks yellowish-green, but it is inert under short-wave ultraviolet light. It exhibits a weak green glow with a fairly long afterglow when irradiated with X-rays.

LOCALITIES AND ROCK TYPES

The best amazonite comes from India. A good-quality amazonite used to be mined in Virginia, but Colorado is now the most important source in the USA. Green material is found in Ontario (Canada), the Ural Mountains in Russia and in the pegmatite masses of Madagascar. Recently, amazonite has been found in the Sahara Desert and in Tanzania and southern Africa.

FASHIONING, IMITATIONS AND SYNTHETICS

Amazonite is cut en cabochon or as beads. Because of the easy cleavage, it is difficult to carve.

| SPECIFIC GRAVITY 2.56 | HARDNESS 6.0–6.5 | CRYSTAL SYSTEM TRICLINIC | DOUBLY REFRACTIVE 1.53 | BIREFRINGENCE 0.008 |

LABRADORITE

PLAGIOCLASE
FELDSPAR GROUP
CHEMICAL COMPOSITION: CALCIUM ALUMINIUM
SILICATE

PHYSICAL AND OPTICAL PROPERTIES

Labradorite has a brilliant play of colour

with blue, green, red, yellow and purple flashes in a grey background. This play of colour or schiller is only seen on a polished surface or near a cleavage plane and is due to the interference of light at the fine layers that are produced by repeated twinning. Platy inclusions of magnetite probably give labradorite the grey colour. The name is derived from Labrador in Canada.

LOCALITIES AND ROCK TYPES

A transparent labradorite from the USA, Mexico and Australia may be almost colourless or pale yellow and does not show a play of colour. A transparent labradorite with a blue flash and needle-like inclusion is found in Madagascar. Other sources include Newfoundland and Quebec, the Ural Mountains and the USA. The variety spectrolite comes from Finland and is similar to the material from Labrador.

FASHIONING, IMITATIONS AND SYNTHETICS

Labradorite is usually carved into decorative boxes, cameos and other *objets d'arts*. Smaller specimens are sometimes made into beads, brooches or ring stones.

| SPECIFIC GRAVITY 2.70 | HARDNESS 6.0–6.5 | CRYSTAL SYSTEM TRICLINIC | DOUBLY REFRACTIVE 1.57 | BIREFRINGENCE 0.006–0.013 |

– PLAGIOCLASE FELDSPARS –

Plagioclase feldspars constitute an isomorphous series with varying chemical composition and consequently varying physical and optical properties. Most form as crystalline masses rather than crystals. From albite to anorthite the density increases.

Albite 90–100% albite with 0–10% anorthite; **Oligoclase** (sunstone) 70–90% albite with 10–30% anorthite; **Andesine** 50–70% albite with 30–50% anorthite; **Labradorite** 30–50% albite with 50–70% anorthite; **Bytownite** 10–30% albite with 70–90% anorthite; **Anorthite** 0–10% albite with 90–100% anorthite

Albite has an ornamental variety called peristerite "pigeon stone". It has a white, cream, fawn or brownish-pink body colour showing a flash of iridescence. The best specimens are found in Canada (Hastings County in Ontario and Quebec). Bytownite has been identified as a reddish faceted stone and a pale yellow bytownite has been found in Oregon in the USA. Andesine resembles jade. Anorthite has been cut for collectors.

SUNSTONE

PLAGIOCLASE
FELDSPAR GROUP
**CHEMICAL COMPOSITION: SODIUM CALCIUM
ALUMINIUM SILICATE**

PHYSICAL AND OPTICAL PROPERTIES
Sunstone, or aventurine, feldspar is a type of oligoclase feldspar. It has reflective inclusions of red, orange or green thin platy crystals of the minerals goethite or hematite, or both, within the almost colourless oligoclase. Repeated twinning is common. Sunstone is inert under ultraviolet light but shows a whitish glow when irradiated with X-rays.

LOCALITIES AND ROCK TYPES
The best source of sunstone is in Norway, where it is found as irregular masses in veins of white quartz in gneiss. Other localities include the area around Lake Baikal in Russia, Ontario (Canada) and southern India. In the USA, sunstone is found in the states of Maine, New Mexico, New York, North Carolina, Pennsylvania and Virginia.

FASHIONING, IMITATIONS AND SYNTHETICS
Sunstone is cut en cabochon.

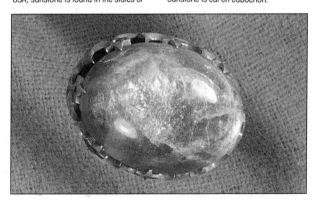

| SPECIFIC GRAVITY 2.64 | HARDNESS 6.0–6.5 | | CRYSTAL SYSTEM **TRICLINIC** | | DOUBLY REFRACTIVE **1.54** | BIREFRINGENCE **0.006–0.013** |

ANDALUSITE

CHEMICAL COMPOSITION: ALUMINIUM SILICATE

PHYSICAL AND OPTICAL PROPERTIES

Andalusite varies in colour from light-yellowish brown to green-brown, light brownish-pink, bottle green or greyish-green. It is named after the Spanish province Andalusia, where the mineral was first found. Andalusite has the same chemical composition as fibrolite, but some of its properties differ. Crystals of andalusite are vertically striated prisms with an almost square cross-section and pyramidal terminations. Crystals are rare, so water-worn pebbles are used for cutting gemstones. Andalusite is very pleochroic and appears yellow, green or red when viewed from different directions. Its lustre is vitreous. Chiastolite is a variety of andalusite which has dark carbonaceous inclusions running across the plane of the prism. When these stones are cut and polished a cross can be seen. Chiastolite is found as long prisms and can be opaque, yellowish or grey.

LOCALITIES AND ROCK TYPES

Gem-quality andalusite is found as dull-green water-worn pebbles in Sri Lankan gem gravels and in stream beds or on slopes of hills under clays and gravel in Brazil. Other localities include Australia, Canada (Quebec), Russia and the USA (California, Maine, Massachusetts and Pennsylvania). Good examples of the chiastolite are found in Burma and Zimbabwe. Other localities for chiastolite include Australia, Bolivia, Chile, France, Spain and the USA.

FASHIONING, IMITATIONS AND SYNTHETICS

Good quality crystals, especially the greenish or reddish varieties, are faceted into gemstones. Chiastolite "cross-stones" are popular in the Pyrenees where they are worn in amulets and charms.

| SPECIFIC GRAVITY 3.15 | HARDNESS 7.5 | | CRYSTAL SYSTEM ORTHORHOMBIC | DOUBLY REFRACTIVE 1.63–1.64 | BIREFRINGENCE 0.010 |

APATITE

CHEMICAL COMPOSITION: **CALCIUM PHOSPHATE WITH SOME FLUORINE OR CHLORINE**

PHYSICAL AND OPTICAL PROPERTIES

Apatite may be colourless, yellow, green, blue or violet. Small gem-quality crystals are found as transparent hexagonal prisms which may be tabular. The crystals are fragile with cleavage parallel to the base. They tend to be transparent to opaque with a vitreous lustre. Some crystals lose their colour when heated and others will fluoresce a bright yellow under ultraviolet light. Apatite has a characteristic absorption spectrum with intense narrow lines due to rare-earth elements. This is seen particularly well in yellow apatite.

LOCALITIES AND ROCK TYPES

Spanish apatite is sometimes called "asparagus stone" because of its yellowish-green colour. Although apatite is found worldwide, the gem-quality material comes mainly from Burma. Blue Burmese apatite is strongly dichroic showing blue and colourless. Sri Lankan apatite comes in various colours. Blue, yellow and green stones are found in Brazil; Norway provides bluish-green stones; Mexico, yellow stones; Bohemia and the USA, violet stones; India, sea-green stones and Canada a deep rich green variety. Other localities include Czechoslovakia and Madagascar.

FASHIONING, IMITATIONS AND SYNTHETICS

Fibrous blue crystals from Burma and Sri Lanka show the cat's-eye effect when cut en cabochon. A massive apatite variety, which is sky-blue in colour, has been polished as an ornamental stone. Apatite is faceted for collectors, but has a hardness of only five on Mohs' scale and so is easily scratched.

SPECIFIC GRAVITY 3.17–3.23 **HARDNESS** 5.0

 CRYSTAL SYSTEM **HEXAGONAL**

 DOUBLY REFRACTIVE **1.63–1.64**

BIREFRINGENCE **0.002–0.004**

AZURITE

CHEMICAL COMPOSITION: COPPER CARBONATE WITH HYDROXIDE

PHYSICAL AND OPTICAL PROPERTIES
Azurite is blue due to the presence of copper in the mineral. It is found as prismatic crystals which may form radiating, botryoidal or stalagmitic groups, or spheres with a silky lustre. It may also occur in massive form. An alternative name for azurite is chessylite after Chessy, near Lyons in France.

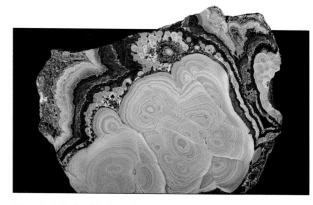

LOCALITIES AND ROCK TYPES
Pure azurite is not usually tough enough to polish or use as a gemstone, but in 1971 some unusually tough azurite was recovered from an old abandoned mine near Las Vegas, USA, called The Copper World Mine. Other localities for azurite include Australia, Namibia, Romania and Siberia.

FASHIONING, IMITATIONS AND SYNTHETICS
Azurite is usually found with malachite. Malachite is an alteration product of azurite which is coloured green by copper. The green and blue of malachite and azurite together in a rock give an attractively banded ornamental stone when polished. Azurite may also be cut en cabochon.

| SPECIFIC GRAVITY 3.77 | HARDNESS 3.5–4.0 | CRYSTAL SYSTEM MONOCLINIC | DOUBLY REFRACTIVE 1.73–1.84 | BIREFRINGENCE 0.110 |

BENITOITE

CHEMICAL COMPOSITION: BARIUM TITANIUM SILICATE

PHYSICAL AND OPTICAL PROPERTIES
Rare blue crystals of benitoite were discovered near San Benito in California (USA) in 1906 by a prospector looking for mercury and copper. He thought the crystals were sapphires but when they were sent to the University of California they were found to be a new mineral and were named after the locality. The crystals are small and resemble flattened triangles in shape. Benitoite has exceptionally strong "fire" (dispersion) which is almost as great as diamond but the blue colour of the stone may mask this. Lustre is vitreous. Benitoite can be distinguished from sapphire because of its obvious dichroism. On turning the

stone the sapphire blue colour is seen in one direction whilst the stone appears colourless when viewed from another. Benitoite is strongly birefringent.

LOCALITIES AND ROCK TYPES
Benitoite is very rare and is only found in the USA (California).

FASHIONING, IMITATIONS AND SYNTHETICS
Blue benitoite has been faceted for collectors. Colourless crystals of benitoite are not uncommon but are not considered worth cutting.

| SPECIFIC GRAVITY 3.65–3.68 | HARDNESS 6.5 | CRYSTAL SYSTEM HEXAGONAL | DOUBLY REFRACTIVE 1.76–1.80 | BIREFRINGENCE 0.047 |

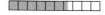

DIOPSIDE

CHEMICAL COMPOSITION: CALCIUM MAGNESIUM SILICATE WITH SOME IRON REPLACING THE MAGNESIUM

PHYSICAL AND OPTICAL PROPERTIES

Most diopside is bottle-green or light green, but colourless, brownish-green and violet-blue stones are also found. The darker stones, some even appearing almost black, are those with more iron and less magnesium in the chemical composition. Crystals are fragile and have perfect prismatic cleavage. They are transparent to translucent with a vitreous lustre. Crystals of the dark violet-blue diopside called violane (spelt violan in the USA) are sometimes found,

but it is more usual to find massive specimens. Star diopside from southern India, which is a dark green to nearly black colour has been on the market since about 1964. They show a four-rayed star which is caused by needle-like inclusions of magnetite. The presence of the magnetite causes these specimens to be magnetic.

LOCALITIES AND ROCK TYPES

Diopside that contains chromium is called chrome diopside. The best specimens are bright green and found in the blue ground of the Kimberley diamond mines of South Africa. Gem-quality chrome diopside is also found in the gem gravels of Sri Lanka, Siberia and

the Hunza region of Pakistan. The Hunza specimens are often large crystals, almost emerald in colour. They may contain fibrous inclusions which give the crystals a cloudy appearance, but these can be cut en cabochon to give an attractive stone. The chrome diopside from Burma is chatoyant. Small bright green crystals are found in California and smoky yellow crystals in Canada.

FASHIONING, IMITATIONS AND SYNTHETICS

Massive specimens (without crystal shape) of violane diopside are polished as beads or used for inlay work. Transparent stones may be faceted, while those with inclusions are cut en cabochon to show the cat's-eye effect.

| SPECIFIC GRAVITY 3.29 | HARDNESS 5.0 | | CRYSTAL SYSTEM **MONOCLINIC** | DOUBLY REFRACTIVE **1.67–1.70** | BIREFRINGENCE **0.030** |

DIOPTASE

CHEMICAL COMPOSITION: COPPER SILICATE

PHYSICAL AND OPTICAL PROPERTIES
The emerald green crystals of dioptase have a strong body colour which masks their good "fire" and makes them translucent rather than transparent. Lustre is vitreous.

LOCALITIES AND ROCK TYPES
Some of the best crystals of dioptase are from Russia. Other localities include the Congo, the copper deposits of the Atacama in Chile, and the USA, particularly Arizona.

FASHIONING, IMITATIONS AND SYNTHETICS
Dioptase is too soft to be used as gemstones and it is only cut, either faceted or en cabochon, for the collector.

SPECIFIC GRAVITY 3.28–3.35 **HARDNESS** 5.0

 CRYSTAL SYSTEM **TRIGONAL**

 DOUBLY REFRACTIVE **1.64–1.71**

BIREFRINGENCE **0.053**

ENSTATITE

CHEMICAL COMPOSITION: MAGNESIUM IRON SILICATE

PHYSICAL AND OPTICAL PROPERTIES
Enstatite is one of the pyroxene minerals. Pyroxenes are a series of minerals with chemical compositions from magnesium silicate to iron silicate. The more iron present in the mineral, the darker the specimen. Too much iron makes the specimen almost opaque and too dark for faceting.

LOCALITIES AND ROCK TYPES
Crystals of enstatite are found as prisms, but gem-quality enstatite is usually found as rolled pebbles. Enstatite of a good green colour is found with diamonds in the blue ground of the South African mines, especially the

Kimberley mine. Brownish-green specimens are found in the Mogok area of Burma, and in Norway and California (USA).

FASHIONING, IMITATIONS AND SYNTHETICS
Bronzite is a dark iron rich enstatite which comes from Austria and can be cut en cabochon to show the cat's-eye effect. Some Sri Lankan grey enstatite is chatoyant.

SPECIFIC GRAVITY 3.27 **HARDNESS** 5.5

 CRYSTAL SYSTEM **ORTHORHOMBIC**

 DOUBLY REFRACTIVE **1.66–1.67**

BIREFRINGENCE **0.009**

FIBROLITE

CHEMICAL COMPOSITION: ALUMINIUM SILICATE

PHYSICAL AND OPTICAL PROPERTIES

Fibrolite is pale blue or green. The name is derived from the fact that it is often fibrous. It is also called sillimanite after Professor Silliman of Yale University, USA. Fibrolite has the same chemical composition as kyanite and andalusite and is therefore polymorphic. Crystals occur in parallel groups as long slender prisms which do not have distinct terminations. Fibrolite has one direction of easy cleavage. Fibrolite shows strong pleochroism, the colours seen down the three principal optical directions are pale green, dark green and blue.

LOCALITIES AND ROCK TYPES

Violet-blue stones are found in Burma, greyish-green stones in Sri Lankan gem gravels and massive fibrous water-worn pebbles in Idaho (USA), which are usually called sillimanite.

FASHIONING, IMITATIONS AND SYNTHETICS

Sri Lankan stones may be cut en cabochon to show the cat's-eye effect.

Sillimanite is commonly fashioned as baroque (irregular-shaped) stones by the tumbling process.

| SPECIFIC GRAVITY 3.25 | HARDNESS 7.5 | CRYSTAL SYSTEM ORTHORHOMBIC | DOUBLY REFRACTIVE 1.66–1.68 | BIREFRINGENCE 0.019 |

– GEMSTONES FOR THE DAYS OF THE WEEK –

Day	Stone
Sunday	Topaz or diamond
Monday	Pearl or crystal
Tuesday	Emerald or ruby
Wednesday	Amethyst or loadstone
Thursday	Carnelian or sapphire
Friday	Emerald or cat's-eye
Saturday	Diamond or turquoise

FLUORITE

CHEMICAL COMPOSITION: CALCIUM FLUORIDE

PHYSICAL AND OPTICAL PROPERTIES

Fluorite occurs in a wide range of colours including colourless, yellow, brown, green, blue, violet and pink. Crystals form as cubes, often with bevelled edges. Twinning is common, and fluorite has perfect octahedral cleavage. The crystals may be coated with other minerals including quartz and pyrite. Lustre is vitreous. Fluorite gets its name from the fact that it fluoresces under ultraviolet light. Most fluorite gives a sky blue to violet glow under long-wave ultraviolet light. Brown fluorite crystals from Clay Center, Ohio (USA), are known to glow white and have a yellow afterglow, said to be due to the inclusion of petroleum or bituminous compounds. Although some fluorite does glow under short-wave ultraviolet light, the colours are generally less striking. Blue John is a massive crystalline variety of fluorite that is more important ornamentally than the crystals. It is inert under ultraviolet light. It is made up of curved bands of blue, violet and purple, which may be so dark as to appear almost black. The purple colour is though to be due to manganese or possibly oil (crude petroleum).

LOCALITIES AND ROCK TYPES

Some of the best crystals are found in England at Weardale in the county of Durham, Alston and Cleator Moor in Cumbria, and in the lead mines of Derbyshire and Cornwall. Fluorite from each mine has a characteristic colour. Pink octahedral crystals can be found near Chamonix, Switzerland. Other localities include the USA (particularly the states of Illinois, New Hampshire and Missouri), Canada, Germany, Czechoslovakia, Poland, Italy and Norway. The only locality for Blue John is the lead mine at Castleton in Derbyshire, England.

FASHIONING, IMITATIONS AND SYNTHETICS

Synthetic material has been made including some pink in colour. Fluorite has a hardness of 4 on Mohs' scale and is therefore too soft to be used in jewellery. The perfect octahedral cleavage makes cutting difficult, but some has been faceted for collectors, usually in the trap-cut style. Blue John has been carved into vases and other decorative objects since Roman times.

SPECIFIC GRAVITY 3.18	HARDNESS 4.0	CRYSTAL SYSTEM **ISOMETRIC**	SINGLY REFRACTIVE **1.43**

IOLITE

CHEMICAL COMPOSITION: **COMPLEX SILICATE OF MAGNESIUM AND ALUMINIUM**

PHYSICAL AND OPTICAL PROPERTIES

The optical and physical values of iolite vary due to the complexity of the composition. Gem-quality iolite is sapphire-blue in colour and has been misnamed "water sapphire" in the past. Non gem-quality crystals are a variety of dark blue to light blue, sometimes with grey as an extra hue.

Iolite is known as cordierite by mineralogists after the French geologist P L A Cordier. The name iolite is derived from the Greek word for violet. Iolite crystals are usually short pseudo-hexagonal prismatic twins. Iolite can be distinguished by its strong pleochroism. The three colours seen are brownish-yellow, light blue and dark blue. The best blue colour is seen when the crystal is viewed down the length of the prism. This physical property gives this stone its third name – dichroite.

Iolite may have various inclusions. The Sri Lankan specimens can contain so many thin platelets of the minerals hematite and goethite that they give the stone a red colour; these stones have been called "bloodshot iolite".

LOCALITIES AND ROCK TYPES

Most gem-quality iolite is found as water-worn pebbles in gem gravels such as those in Sri Lanka and Burma. Other localities for gem material include Madagascar, India and Canada. Good iolite is found in Namibia and Tanzania.

FASHIONING, IMITATIONS AND SYNTHETICS

Most iolite is faceted though massive grey iolite, which looks rather like grey jadeite, makes a decorative stone for carving.

SPECIFIC GRAVITY 2.57–2.66 **HARDNESS** 7.0

 CRYSTAL SYSTEM **ORTHORHOMBIC**

 DOUBLY REFRACTIVE **1.53–1.55**

BIREFRINGENCE **0.008–0.012**

KORNERUPINE

CHEMICAL COMPOSITION: MAGNESIUM IRON ALUMINIUM BOROSILICATE

PHYSICAL AND OPTICAL PROPERTIES

Kornerupine is a rare mineral which may be green, brownish-green or yellow. The mineral was first found in Greenland, where it is scarce and of no use as a gemstone. It was named in 1884 in memory of A N Kornerup, a young Danish scientist. The strong pleochroism is a characteristic feature and the two colours are green and reddish-brown.

LOCALITIES AND ROCK TYPES

Kornerupine is found as rolled pebbles, in gem gravels for example, rather than crystals. Gem-quality green stones were found in 1912 in Madagascar and in 1936 brownish-green stones were found in Sri Lanka. Green kornerupine has been found in the Mogok area of Burma. The fine green colour of kornerupine found Ir Kenya and Tanzania is due to the presence of a small amount of the element vanadium.

FASHIONING, IMITATIONS AND SYNTHETICS

To obtain the best colour the stones should be cut with the table facet parallel to the length of the crystal. Small dark cabochon, are found in Sri Lanka. Gem-quality kornerupine is rare but has been faceted for collectors of the unusual.

SPECIFIC GRAVITY 3.32   **HARDNESS** 6.5

 CRYSTAL SYSTEM **ORTHORHOMBIC**   DOUBLY REFRACTIVE **1.66–1.68**   BIREFRINGENCE **0.013**

MALACHITE

CHEMICAL COMPOSITION: **HYDRATED COPPER CARBONATE**

The name malachite may be derived from its colour or its softness – it measures only 4 on Mohs' scale – since there are two Greek words which could give its origin: *malache*, which means mallow and *malakos*, which means soft. During the Middle Ages, malachite was thought to protect small children from danger and illness.

PHYSICAL AND OPTICAL PROPERTIES

Malachite is opaque and ranges in colour from weak green to emerald-green and from deep, dark green to blackish-green. The colour is due to the presence of copper. The compact monoclinic crystals, which occur in microcrystalline masses, are usually nodules with radiating bands. Malachite is usually found intergrown with the blue mineral azurite. It may also be found with the minerals turquoise and chrysocolla to give what is called Eilat stone. When slabs of malachite are polished the distinctive banding of different shades of green give a very attractive ornamental stone with a silky lustre.

LOCALITIES AND ROCK TYPES

Much of the older malachite used in jewellery was from copper mines in the Ural Mountains of Russia. Malachite suitable for cutting is also found in Queensland, New South Wales and South Australia, where it is found with azurite. Other localities include the USA and the copper-mining areas of Africa, including Zaire, Zambia and Zimbabwe.

FASHIONING, IMITATIONS AND SYNTHETICS

The ancient Egyptians, Romans and Greeks all used malachite for jewellery. Malachite can be cut en cabochon, as beads for jewellery or carved.

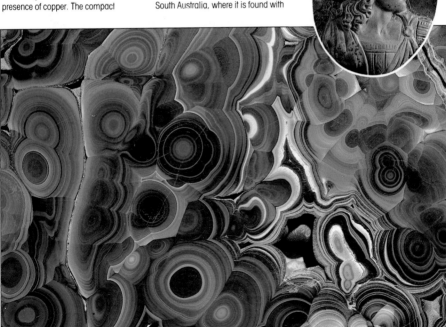

SPECIFIC GRAVITY 3.80 (mean) HARDNESS 4.0

 CRYSTAL SYSTEM **MONOCLINIC**

 DOUBLY REFRACTIVE **1.85 (mean)**

RHODO-CHROSITE

CHEMICAL COMPOSITION: **MANGANESE CARBONATE**

PHYSICAL AND OPTICAL PROPERTIES
Rhodochrosite has a distinctive pale pink colour and makes an attractive ornamental stone with bands of slightly differing shades of pink. Grey, fawn and brown banded rhodochrosite is also found, but is less attractive than the pink.

LOCALITIES AND ROCK TYPES
Rhodochrosite is found as rhombohedral crystals and in granular masses. There are many localities but few have rhodochrosite that is good enough to be used as a decorative stone. One of the oldest localities is thought to be Argentina, where it is called "inca rose".

Colorado and Montana in the USA are commercial sources of decorative rhodochrosite. Romania, Hungary, India and Germany are also sources of rhodochrosite but not in commercial quantities.

FASHIONING, IMITATIONS AND SYNTHETICS
In 1974, attractive transparent crystals of rhodochrosite were discovered in the Kalahari Desert region of South Africa, which were cut to give stones for collectors only.

SPECIFIC GRAVITY 3.50–3.60 HARDNESS 4.0

CRYSTAL SYSTEM **TRIGONAL**

DOUBLY REFRACTIVE **1.60–1.80**

BIREFRINGENCE **0.220**

RHODONITE

CHEMICAL COMPOSITION: **MANGANESE SILICATE WITH SOME CALCIUM**

PHYSICAL AND OPTICAL PROPERTIES
Rhodonite has a rose-red colour and is mostly opaque to translucent. The colour is due to the presence of manganese. Rhodonite has a distinct cleavage, uneven fracture and is brittle. It takes a good polish and makes an attractive decorative stone.

LOCALITIES AND ROCK TYPES
Rhodonite is found in the Urals of Russia as massive material rather like marble. The pink is veined by black where manganese has been oxidized during weathering. Other localities include Sweden, USA, Mexico, South Africa, Australia and Cornwall in England.

FASHIONING, IMITATIONS AND SYNTHETICS
Most translucent rhodonite is fashioned into beads and cabochons for ornamental articles and as inlay. Transparent rhodonite is rare, but has been faceted for collectors.

SPECIFIC GRAVITY 3.50–3.70 HARDNESS 6.0

CRYSTAL SYSTEM **TRICLINIC**

DOUBLY REFRACTIVE **near 1.72**

SCAPOLITE

CHEMICAL COMPOSITION: ALUMINIUM SILICATE WITH CALCIUM AND SODIUM

PHYSICAL AND OPTICAL PROPERTIES

Scapolite is part of a continuous compositional series from calcium-rich to sodium-rich. Scapolite is found as white, pink, violet, blue and yellow stones. Crystals are prismatic with three directions of easy cleavage. Scapolite's lustre varies from vitreous to resinous. The name scapolite comes from the Greek for "stick stone", which refers to the habit in which the crystal is usually found, i.e. as prismatic crystals.

LOCALITIES AND ROCK TYPES

Gem material was first found in the Mogok area of Burma as fibrous white, pink or violet stones. The pink and violet stones have strong pleochroism, showing dark blue and lavender blue, and can be cut en cabochon to show the cat's-eye effect. Yellow stones have been found in Brazil and Madagascar. These show strong pleochroism; the colours are three shades of yellow. An opaque massive yellow variety of scapolite is found in Quebec and Ontario, Canada, which emits a brilliant yellow fluorescence under long-wave ultraviolet light and may be cut en cabochon.

Colourless, purple and gem-quality yellow scapolite has been found in Kenya.

FASHIONING, IMITATIONS AND SYNTHETICS

The Burmese scapolite is cut en cabochon to show the cat's-eye effect, while the Brazilian yellow scapolite is usually faceted.

SPECIFIC GRAVITY 2.60–270 HARDNESS 6.0

| | CRYSTAL SYSTEM **TETRAGONAL** | DOUBLY REFRACTIVE **1.54–1.58** | BIREFRINGENCE **0.010** |

SERPENTINE

CHEMICAL COMPOSITION: **HYDRATED MAGNESIUM SILICATE**

PHYSICAL AND OPTICAL PROPERTIES

Massive serpentine can be divided into those stones that can be carved, such as the bowenite variety and the softer types which are of little use as decorative stones. The name serpentine may have been derived from its ancient use as a cure for snake or serpent bite, or it may be because the green and mottled appearance of the stone is similar to that of some snake skins.

The bowenite variety of serpentine, which is a translucent green, is sometimes used as an alternative to jade as it has a similar appearance and may be referred to as "new jade". Bowenite is named after a Dr Bowen who originally misidentified bowenite as nephrite jade. Williamsite is another variety of serpentine. It is an oil-green colour, softer than bowenite and contains black inclusions.

LOCALITIES AND ROCK TYPES

Italian serpentines vary from green to brownish-red in colour and often the material is veined with a white mineral. In England the best known serpentine rock comes from the Lizard peninsula of Cornwall. Colours vary and may be green, red, purple, brown, nearly black or white, and may be veined or spotted with as many colours. The serpentine is used to make gifts for tourists. Other sources of serpentine that are used for carving include Wales, Scotland, Austria, France, Germany, South Africa and the USA.

FASHIONING, IMITATIONS AND SYNTHETICS

China is the main exporter of figurines carved from yellowish-green bowenite which often contains cloudy patches. Dark green or bluish-green bowenite found in the South Island of New Zealand was used by the Maoris, who called it *tangiwai* meaning "tears", but little is found today. A coarser green bowenite from the USA was also used in the past. Bowenite is also found in Afghanistan where it is used to make dagger hilts, knife handles, caskets, amulets and other articles.

SPECIFIC GRAVITY 2.58–2.59 HARDNESS 2.5

 CRYSTAL SYSTEM **MONOCLINIC**

 DOUBLY REFRACTIVE **1.56 (mean)**

SINHALITE

CHEMICAL COMPOSITION: MAGNESIUM ALUMINIUM IRON BORATE

PHYSICAL AND OPTICAL PROPERTIES
Sinhalite varies from pale yellow-brown to dark greenish-brown in colour. The name is derived from *Sinhala*, the Sanskrit name for Sri Lanka. Until 1952 sinhalite was thought to be a brown coloured peridot, but it was noticed that the density was slightly higher, and X-ray crystallography showed that sinhalite was a new mineral. Sinhalite has distinct pleochroism showing the colours pale brown, greenish-brown and dark brown.

LOCALITIES AND ROCK TYPES
Most gem-quality sinhalite is found as rolled pebbles in the gem gravels of Sri Lanka. A crystal has been known to have come from Burma, but this is particularly rare. Sinhalite has also been found in Warren County, New York (USA) but this is not of gem-quality.

FASHIONING, IMITATIONS AND SYNTHETICS
Gem-quality sinhalite is faceted.

SPECIFIC GRAVITY 3.48   **HARDNESS** 6.5

 CRYSTAL SYSTEM **ORTHORHOMBIC**   DOUBLY REFRACTIVE **1.67–1.71**   BIREFRINGENCE **0.038**

SODALITE

CHEMICAL COMPOSITION: SODIUM ALUMINIUM SILICATE WITH SODIUM CHLORIDE

PHYSICAL AND OPTICAL PROPERTIES
Sodalite has a rich blue colour and is one of the components of the rock lapis lazuli. Sodalite is a darker blue colour and has a lower density than lapis lazuli and it rarely contains the brassy specks of the mineral pyrite that are found in lapis lazuli.

LOCALITIES AND ROCK TYPES
Sodalite was found in Canada during a Royal visit and was called "Princess Blue". It is also known as "Canadian Blue Stone" or just "Bluestone". The major commercial source in Canada is in Hastings County, Ontario. Sodalite is also found in Norway, the USA, Brazil and Namibia.

FASHIONING, IMITATIONS AND SYNTHETICS
Sodalite is fashioned as cabochons and beads, and is cut and polished into slabs for use as inlays in clock cases, cigarette boxes and other items.

SPECIFIC GRAVITY 2.15–2.35   **HARDNESS** 5.5–6.0

 CRYSTAL SYSTEM **ISOMETRIC**   SINGLY REFRACTIVE **1.48**

SPHENE

CHEMICAL COMPOSITION: SILICATE OF TITANIUM AND CALCIUM

PHYSICAL AND OPTICAL PROPERTIES
Gem-quality sphene is yellow, brown or green. Titanite is the correct mineralogical name for this gem. Crystals are found as wedge shapes and are often twinned. They are brittle and have a weak cleavage. Sphene has very high "fire" and the birefringence is high enough for doubling of the back facets to be seen with ease.

LOCALITIES AND ROCK TYPES
Major localities for sphene are the Austrian Tyrol and Swiss Grisons, and also Canada and Madagascar. Other sources include Burma, Baja California, Brazil and Sri Lanka.

FASHIONING, IMITATIONS AND SYNTHETICS
Sphene is usually cut as brilliant or mixed cut gems to show the "fire" to its best effect.

SPECIFIC GRAVITY 3.52–3.54 HARDNESS 5.5		CRYSTAL SYSTEM **MONOCLINIC**	DOUBLY REFRACTIVE **1.88–2.05**	BIREFRINGENCE **0.105–0.135**

SPODUMENE

CHEMICAL COMPOSITION: LITHIUM ALUMINIUM SILICATE

PHYSICAL AND OPTICAL PROPERTIES
Kunzite and hiddenite are both varieties of spodumene. The name spodumene is derived from the Greek meaning "burnt to ashes". Kunzite is lilac-pink in colour and has strong pleochroism, showing colourless and two shades of violet. Hiddenite is bright green, coloured by chromium. Hiddenite is pleochroic, showing bluish-green, emerald green and yellowish-green, and has a characteristic chromium absorption spectrum. Spodumene occurs as flattened prisms characterized by vertical striations and irregular terminations. The crystals exhibit strong cleavage in two directions.

LOCALITIES AND ROCK TYPES
Spodumene was discovered in 1877 in Brazil. Emerald-green hiddenite and lilac-coloured kunzite have been found in the USA. Other spodumene localities include Madagascar and Burma.

FASHIONING, IMITATIONS AND SYNTHETICS
Cutting is difficult because of the strong cleavage and the shape of the crystals. Because of the strong pleochroism the stones should be cut to show the best colour through the front of the stone.

SPECIFIC GRAVITY 3.18	HARDNESS 7.0		CRYSTAL SYSTEM **MONOCLINIC**	DOUBLY REFRACTIVE **1.66–1.68**	BIREFRINGENCE **0.015**

TAAFFEITE

CHEMICAL COMPOSITION: BERYLLIUM MAGNESIUM ALUMINIUM OXIDE

PHYSICAL AND OPTICAL PROPERTIES
Taaffeite is an extremely rare mineral which is of interest as it is the first mineral to have been identified when already cut as a gemstone. The first specimen was found in 1945 by Count Taaffe of Dublin amongst a jeweller's box of mixed stones. The pale mauve stone weighing 1.419 carats resembled spinel but was doubly refractive whereas spinel is singly refractive. A second taaffeite specimen (0.86 carats) was found in 1949 and a third in 1957; since then only a few more have been found including a ruby-red specimen and a sapphire-blue.

LOCALITIES AND ROCK TYPES
Taaffeite specimens have been found in Sri Lanka, China and Russia.

FASHIONING, IMITATIONS AND SYNTHETICS
Taaffeites are usually faceted as round brilliants. It is not imitated or synthesized.

| SPECIFIC GRAVITY 3.62 | HARDNESS 8.0 | | CRYSTAL SYSTEM HEXAGONAL | | DOUBLY REFRACTIVE 1.72–1.73 | BIREFRINGENCE 0.005 |

ZOISITE

CHEMICAL COMPOSITION: CALCIUM ALUMINIUM SILICATE WITH HYDROXIDE

PHYSICAL AND OPTICAL PROPERTIES
The best gem-quality zoisite crystals are called tanzanite. The transparent blue crystals with vitreous lustre are the most attractive for use in jewellery. Blue, green, yellow, pink or brown zoisite all change colour to blue when heated. Zoisite has one perfect plane of cleavage and shows distinct pleochroism. Thulite is a massive pink variety of zoisite named after *Thule*, the ancient name for Norway.

LOCALITIES AND ROCK TYPES
Tanzanite and a massive green chrome-rich variety of zoisite, which contains hexagonal rubies, are found in Tanzania.

Thulite is found in Norway, the Austrian Tyrol, Western Australia and the USA (North Carolina).

FASHIONING, IMITATIONS AND SYNTHETICS
Zoisite found with parallel fibres shows a cat's-eye effect when cut en cabochon. Massive green zoisite has been fashioned complete with rubies as ashtrays and small objects. Thulite is used as an ornamental stone.

| SPECIFIC GRAVITY 3.35 | HARDNESS 6.5 | | CRYSTAL SYSTEM ORTHORHOMBIC | | DOUBLY REFRACTIVE 1.69–1.70 | BIREFRINGENCE 0.009 |

OBSIDIAN

NATURAL GLASS

CHEMICAL COMPOSITION: NATURAL GLASS MAINLY SILICA

PHYSICAL AND OPTICAL PROPERTIES

Natural glasses do not belong to any of the seven crystal symmetry systems since they are amorphous, i.e. do not have a crystalline structure. Obsidian is the best known of the natural glasses. It is named after Obsius, the man who first found a stone of this type, who was mentioned by the Roman writer Pliny. Obsidian may be brown, black or grey and, very rarely, green, red or blue. Inclusions of gold or silver-coloured minerals give a metallic sheen and other colours show as iridescence. Obsidian itself has a vitrous lustre. Crystallites are crystalline inclusions Obsidian may have white marks like snowflakes ("snowflake obsidian"), contain bubbles, or have red or brown banding.

LOCALITIES AND ROCK TYPES

Obsidian is found throughout the world where volcanic activity occurs or has occurred in the past (for instance Hawaii, Japan, Iceland and the Lipari islands off Italy). It is formed by the rapid cooling of volcanic lava which allows no time for crystals to form. There is no cleavage, but fracture is shell-like (conchoidal). Most of the obsidian used in jewellery comes form the USA and South America (Mexico, Guatemala and Equador). Arizona, Colorado and Nevada have deposits of obsidian, and California has many sites where the material has been quarried from ancient times. Glassy, pebble-like solid lumps of obsidian are found in New Mexico and are called "Apache tears".

FASHIONING, IMITATIONS AND SYNTHETICS

Obsidian is carved or cut en cabochon. Iridescent obsidian from Oregon was used by the American Indians to make arrowheads. In Mexico, the Incas used obsidian for weapons, mirrors, masks and earrings.

SPECIFIC GRAVITY 2.33–2.42 **HARDNESS** 5.0

 CRYSTAL SYSTEM **AMORPHOUS**

 REFRACTIVE INDEX 1.48–1.51

TEKTITES

NATURAL GLASS
CHEMICAL COMPOSITION: MAINLY SILICA WITH SOME ALUMINIUM AND IRON OXIDES

PHYSICAL AND OPTICAL PROPERTIES

Tektites are natural glasses of unknown origin. Tektites are transparent green, greenish-brown or brown in colour, and have a bobbly or craggy surface. One theory suggests that the characteristic shape of tektites is due to the fact that they were still molten as they travelled through the atmosphere from outer space. Alternatively, tektites may be the scattered drops of molten rock thrown out by the impact of a large meteorite. The name comes from the Greek word *tektos* meaning molten.

SOURCES

Moldavites are a type of tektite named after the river in Czechoslovakia where these glassy pieces were first found in 1787. Pieces of tektite from other localities have also been named after the place where they were found. For example, billitonites from Billiton Island, now called Belitung, in Indonesia, australites from Australia and Georgiaites from Georgia in the USA.

FASHIONING, IMITATIONS AND SYNTHETICS

Moldavites have been faceted as gemstones and look similar to the bottle green mineral peridot. They contain round or torpedo-shaped bubbles and characteristic swirls like treacle. These are easily distinguished from the swirls in paste (glass) since there are no crystalline inclusions as there are in volcanic obsidian. Other forms of tektites are carved into small decorative objects.

SPECIFIC GRAVITY 2.34–2.39 **HARDNESS** 5.0

CRYSTAL SYSTEM **AMORPHOUS**

REFRACTIVE INDEX **1.49–1.50**

AMBER

ORGANICS

CHEMICAL COMPOSITION: **COMPLEX MIXTURE OF RESINS, SUCCINIC ACID AND A VOLATILE OIL**

PHYSICAL AND OPTICAL PROPERTIES

Amber is a fossil resin thought to have come from pine trees. The Greek name for amber was *electron*, as rubbing produces a negative charge on the amber which attracts small particles.

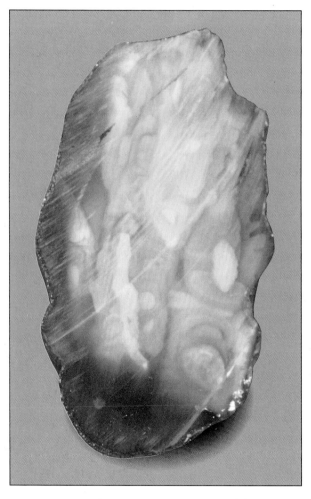

Amber is transparent to translucent and has a greasy lustre. Its colour is typically yellow or brown but it may have a red or white tinge. Amber is often cloudy, due to air spaces. Heating cloudy material in oil fills the air spaces and clears the amber. Insects, for example flies, pieces of moss, lichens and pine needles can be found trapped in amber, which was once a soft, sticky resin. Pyrite crystals and calcite have also been seen as inclusions in amber.

SOURCES

The main localities for amber are along the Samland Coast near Kaliningrad, Russia. Pit amber is obtained by open-pit mining. The amber is separated from the soft sandy deposits using strong jets of water. Sea amber, which has been washed out from the sea bed, floats on water and is carried by the tides and currents to the shorelines of the Baltic, Norway, Denmark and England. The variety from the Baltic is called succinite. The Burmese variety (burmite) found in clayey soil, is much redder than the Baltic variety and is harder and denser. Sicilian amber is called simetite after the name of the river along which it is found. Amber is also found in the Dominican Republic, Romania, Czechoslovakia, Germany, Canada and the USA.

FASHIONING, IMITATIONS AND SYNTHETICS

Amber is valued for jewellery and ornaments since it is readily carved and takes a high polish. Pieces that are too small to work are pressed together under gentle heat to form a larger piece which is called ambroid.

Amber can be imitated by plastic, glass and a resin called copal from the kauri pine trees of New Zealand. However, the artificial product fails to produce the pleasant aroma which natural amber yields when rubbed.

SPECIFIC GRAVITY 1.08

HARDNESS 2.5

 CRYSTAL SYSTEM **AMORPHOUS**

JET

ORGANICS
CHEMICAL COMPOSITION: HYDROCARBON

PHYSICAL AND OPTICAL PROPERTIES

Jet is a variety of coal. It is a fossil wood which formed when wood rotted in stagnant water and was then flattened by the pressure of burial over millions of years. It smells like coal when burnt or when touched with a hot needle. Some jet may induce electricity when rubbed and for this reason it is sometimes known as "black amber". The name is derived from the old French *jyet* or *jaiet*

after a place on the Mediterranean coast where the Romans obtained some of their jet.

LOCALITIES AND ROCK TYPES

There is evidence that jet was mined as early as 1400BC and during the Roman occupation of the British Isles jet was shipped to Rome. It was a popular gem during Victorian times when it was used for mourning jewellery and the town of Whitby on the Yorkshire coast, England received much of its income from the jet industry at this time. Jet for use in jewellery has also been mined in

Asturias, Spain. Other sources include Aude in France, Utah in the USA, Germany and Russia, but these have not been systematically worked.

FASHIONING, IMITATIONS AND SYNTHETICS

Jet has an intense black colour and can take a good polish. Beads, pendants and charms made of jet have been found in early burial mounds which pre-date written history.

Coal, rubber, glass, obsidian, black stained chalcedony and plastics have all been used to imitate jet. "Paris jet" is a black glass.

SPECIFIC GRAVITY 1.30–1.35 **HARDNESS** 2.5–4.0

IVORY

ORGANICS

CHEMICAL COMPOSITION: **CALCIUM PHOSPHATE**
(DENTINE)

PHYSICAL AND OPTICAL PROPERTIES

Ivory is a constituent of the teeth or tusks of all mammals. It has a rich creamy colour and fine texture and is almost perfectly elastic. The best African elephant ivory has a warm transparent mellow tint with little grain or mottling. Indian elephants have smaller tusks than African elephants and the ivory is a denser white, more open in texture, softer to work and yellows more easily. The ivory of the incisor and canine teeth of the hippopotamus is denser than elephant ivory. The exterior of walrus ivory has a much finer texture and grain than the core. The narwhal is a species of whale; the male narwahals have an incisor tooth that may be over 2m/6½ft long. It looks like a spiralled, twisted tusk and has been sold as "unicorn horn". The ivory of the boar and warthog is taken from their strong, curved teeth

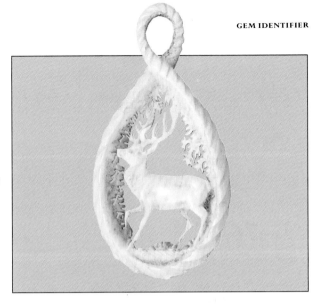

and is coarse with a consistency more like bone than true ivory. The cachalot whale, or sperm whale, has curved conical teeth with ivory similar to that of the boar. Most ivories fluoresce with a bluish glow under ultraviolet light. The coarser the ivory, the darker the shade of blue.

SOURCES
Indian and African elephant tusks (recent and fossil), tusks of the walrus, narwhal (found in the Arctic) and boar, and the teeth of the hippopotamus and sperm whale are all sources of ivory.

FASHIONING, IMITATIONS AND SYNTHETICS
Ordinary wood carving chisels can be used to carve ivory which, unlike bone, requires no preparation before fashioning. Carvings on mammoth ivory estimated to be about 30,000 years old have been found in caves in France. Ornamental carvings from China and Europe have been known since the thirteenth century. It was the aim of the craftsman to keep the original shape of the ivory piece as far as possible, however odd the shape. In Japan, ivory is considered a precious material and is used for ornamental buttons (netsukes) and other decorative and functional articles. The almost-perfect elasticity of ivory makes it an ideal medium for billiard balls, fine-toothed combs, piano keys, precision scales and rulers. Now that there are international restrictions on the ivory trade, plastics and other materials are being introduced in its place. Ivory can be imitated by bone, deer-horn and vegetable ivory. Vegetable ivory includes the hard seeds, or nuts of palm trees such as the ivory plam which grows in Peru and the doom palm of central Africa.

SPECIFIC GRAVITY 1.70–1.90 **HARDNESS** 2.5

– LINES OF RETZIUS –

Elephant ivory can be recognized by the "lines of Retzius", which are a pattern of criss-crossing lines. These are due to the fine thread-like canals filled with a brownish gelatinous substance, which in life conducted delicate nerve fibres. Under a microscope the thread-like canals can be seen to form a wave-like pattern of lines crossing at right angles. In hippopotamus ivory the undulating pattern is much finer, while in walrus and narwhal ivory it is much coarser with more ramification of the canals. In boar and whale teeth the canals appear straighter and are somewhat radial from the centre of the tooth.

CORAL

ORGANICS
CHEMICAL COMPOSITION: **CALCIUM CARBONATE OR CONCHIOLIN**

PHYSICAL AND OPTICAL PROPERTIES

Coral polyps are marine organisms related to sea anemones. They have a hollow cylindrical body with a ring of tentacles around the mouth and secrete an external chalky or horny skeleton. Red, pink, white and blue corals are made of calcium carbonate, while black and golden corals are formed of a horny substance called conchiolin. The polyps usually exist in large colonies and form the united, branching masses we know as coral. The coral grows as the polyps ingest small animals and plants and secrete more of the skeleton-forming substances. Japanese precious coral is red, pink or white. Red coral (*Corallium rubrum*) and white coral (*Oculinacea vaseuclosa*) have been fashioned for ornamentation. Black coral, known as "Akabar" or "King's coral" (*Antipathes spiralis*), and blue coral, known as "Akori" coral (*Allopara subirolcea*), are two other varieties. All corals have the distinctive, delicate graining of stripes or spots as a result of the skeletal structure.

SOURCES

Most coral types prefer warm temperatures and are therefore restricted to the warm waters of the world including the Italian and African Mediterranean coasts, where red and pink corals are found, the Red Sea and the waters off Malaysia and Japan. Black and golden coral are found off Hawaii, Australia and the West Indies.

FASHIONING, IMITATIONS AND SYNTHETICS

Coral is cut en cabochon or carved and fashioned into beads, small carved objects and cameos.
Coral has been imitated by stained vegetable ivory, mixtures of rubber and the mineral gypsum, stained bone, glass, porcelain and plastic.
Gilson "Created" coral is manufactured in a laboratory by crushing and staining the mineral calcite. It has a similar colour, lustre and general appearance to coral, but can be distinguished using a hand lens; the Gilson "Created" coral appears quite homogenous in contrast to the true coral, which has a "wood-grain" structure.

SPECIFIC GRAVITY 2.60–2.70 **HARDNESS** 3.5

TORTOISE-SHELL

ORGANICS
CHEMICAL COMPOSITION: **PROTEIN (KERATIN)**

PHYSICAL AND OPTICAL PROPERTIES

Tortoiseshell is not the shell from a tortoise, but the carapace (shield) of a sea turtle called the Hawksbill turtle. It is made of a protein which is similar to that in animal horns, claws and nails. The shell has a rich brown mottling on a warm translucent yellow background. Under a microscope the mottling can be seen as spherical spots of colour. It can be distinguished from imitations such as plastic which appears as patches or swathes of colour rather than dots or spots when viewed with a microscope.

Tortoiseshell gives off a characteristic smell of burning hair when touched by a hot needle.

SOURCES

The Hawksbill turtle is found in the seas of Indonesia.

FASHIONING, IMITATIONS AND SYNTHETICS

To fashion the shells they must first be flattened using low heat and the ridges removed by scraping. Sheets can be pressed together using heat, being careful not to overheat as this darkens the colour. The shell is then polished and cut. In Roman times one use for tortoiseshell was as inlay for furniture. This practice was popular in France but is now seldom used. Nowadays plastic is usually used in place of tortoiseshell.

SPECIFIC GRAVITY 1.29   **HARDNESS** 2.5

SHELL

ORGANICS
CHEMICAL COMPOSITION: **CALCIUM CARBONATE**

PHYSICAL AND OPTICAL PROPERTIES

The shell of the giant conch (*Strombus gigas*) is a layered material which is carved as cameos to show the two distinct colours of pink and white. The pink layer fades with excess strong light. Helmet shells (*Cassis madagascariensis*) are also used for cameo work. Some shells, such as the large pearl oysters (*Pinctada maxima* and *Pinctada margaritifera*) have an iridescent lustre to their lining called mother-of-pearl. Shells with brightly coloured blue and green shell, called paua shells and abalones, are fished for their mother-of-pearl. The larger topshells (*Trocus*) are also fished for the value of their shell.

SOURCES

Helmet shells are found in the warm waters of the West Indies. The *Pinctada* oysters are found off northern Australia. Abalones are found in American waters and paua shells in New Zealand.

FASHIONING, IMITATIONS AND SYNTHETICS

Shells are normally carved, especially into cameos. Mother-of-pearl is used for making buttons, knife handles, inlay and other ornaments. The thick column of topshells is sometimes turned into beads and strung as necklaces.

SPECIFIC GRAVITY 1.08   **HARDNESS** 2.0

PEARL

O R G A N I C S

CHEMICAL COMPOSITION: CALCIUM CARBONATE, CONCHIOLIN AND WATER

PHYSICAL AND OPTICAL PROPERTIES

Any shelled mollusc can produce pearls, but only those animals which have a shell with a pearly (nacreous) lining can form lustrous pearls worth using as ornamentation. The animals which produce the pearls most used in jewellery are molluscs of the *Pinctada* type and all live in sea-water. Other sea-water molluscs that produce pearls include the giant conch (*Strombus gigas*) and giant clam (*Tridacna gigas*). "Scotch pearls" are found in fresh-water molluscs in Scottish rivers.

Blister pearls form when a piece of grit or other irritant gets between the shell and the soft outer body parts of the mollusc (mantle). The mollusc secretes nacre to ease the irritation. The bulge or blister that this forms can be scraped off the shell and used in jewellery. Blister pearls are mounted so that the non-nacreous base is hidden.

True pearls are formed by encystation and are termed "cyst" pearls. The mollusc is unable to cover the irritant against the shell and instead it envelops it within the mantle. The irritant forms a dent in the mantle which becomes a sac surrounding the irritant. During the next stage the sac separates from the mantle and a cyst is formed. The nacre-secreting cells of the pearl sac continue to secret nacre around the irritant and these concentric layers gradually build up to form the pearl.

The lustre of pearls is known as the "orient of pearl". It is due to the optical effects of diffraction and interference. Light is diffracted by the irregular overlapping crystals of aragonite that make up the pearl and there is also interference at these platelets.

SOURCES

Fresh-water pearls are fished from rivers in Europe and the USA. Sea-water pearls are fished from the Persian Gulf, the Gulf of Manaar in the Indian Ocean, the Red Sea, to the north-west Australian coast and the Gulf of California and Florida. The colour and surface texture of the pearls is partly dependent upon the type of shellfish and local conditions.

FASHIONING, IMITATIONS AND SYNTHETICS

A cross-section of a nucleated cultured pearl shows the bead at the centre with

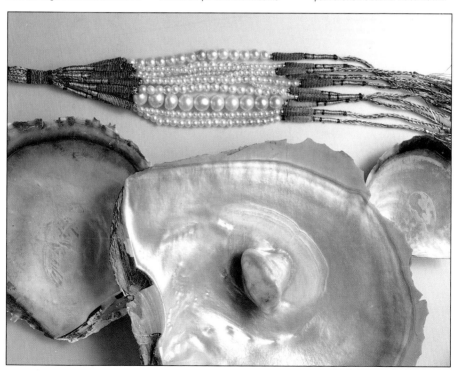

parallel markings of the shell surrounded by a thin amount of the concentric layered nacre. A true pearl has the concentric layering without the parallel markings. The internal structure can be distinguished without cutting the pearl by passing X-rays through the pearl onto photographic paper and interpreting the pattern. An instrument called an endoscope is used to shine light through the drill hole of the pearls. The resulting reflections are used to distinguish between true and cultivated pearls. Pearls have been imitated by pressed fish scales (pearl essence) and by glass and plastic beads which have been covered with pearl essence. Using a hand lens the pearl essence surface looks like tissue paper rather than having the uneven serrated surface of a natural pearl.

SPECIFIC GRAVITY 2.60–2.78 **HARDNESS** 3.5

– CULTIVATED PEARLS –

In many areas over-fishing has led to a decline in the production of natural pearls. Japan has overcome this problem by cultivating pearls. Cultured pearls have been used in jewellery by the Chinese for centuries; small objects, such as metal figures of the Buddha, were inserted between the shell and the mantle. These were subsequently covered by nacre to form a blister pearl in the shape of the Buddha.

The pearl-producing mollusc most used in Japan is the small oyster *Pinctada martensi*. Once the oysters reach a certain age or size they are collected and an irritant (usually a small spherical bead of mother-of-pearl) is carefully added before replacing the still-living oysters back in the water. The bead acts as the nucleus around which the pearl forms. Non-nucleated pearls have been cultivated by using a small amount of soft tissue from one oyster and grafting it on to another where it forms a sufficient irritant for pearl growth.

GLOSSARY

....

Absorption spectrum – is the pattern of dark lines seen when white light is examined by a spectroscope after the light has passed through a gemstone. Spectral colours can be absorbed by impurities and defects in the gem and dark bands are seen in the resulting spectrum.

Amorphous – means "without shape". Amorphous substances have no regular internal structure, i.e. they are not crystalline.

Asterism – is the star effect seen in a gemstone when cut and polished *en cabochon.*

Birefringence – where large, is seen as the apparent doubling of the back facets of a gem. It is calculated as the difference between the maximum and minimum *refractive indices* of a *doubly refractive* stone.

Cabochon – is a style of cutting used for opaque gemstones or to show *asterism* or chatoyancy (cat's-eye effect). The stone is polished with a smooth domed surface.

Cleavage – is the tendency of a stone to break along a definite direction giving a smooth surface. The plane of cleavage is due to a weakness within the atomic structure (see *Fracture*).

Conchoidal fracture – is an uneven breaking of a stone which gives a shell-like appearance to the surface.

Cryptocrystalline – crystals are so small that they can only be seen with the aid of a microscope.

Crystal – a form bounded by flat *faces*. The external shape of the crystal is directly related to its internal atomic structure.

Dichroism – see *Pleochroism.*

Diffraction – is the splitting of white light into the colours of the rainbow (spectral colours) as light passes through narrow slits, for example in a spectroscope.

Dispersion – is the splitting of white light into the spectral colours when it passes through a gemstone. It is also known as "fire".

Dodecahedron – a solid figure with twelve faces.

Doubly refractive – describes a gemstone which refracts different rays of light by different amounts to give a range of *refractive indices.*

Faces – are the flat external surfaces which make up a crystal.

Facets – are the flat surfaces of a cut and polished gemstone.

Fluorescence – in a gemstone is the emission of visible light when the stone is exposed to invisible light such as ultraviolet light or X-rays.

Form – describes a number of identical flat *faces* that make up a crystal. More than one form may be needed to describe a crystal.

Fracture – is the uneven breaking of a stone. The direction of breaking is not related to the atomic structure of the stone (see *Cleavage*).

Habit – is the form in which a gemstone is usually found.

Icositetrahedron – is a solid figure with 20 four-sided faces.

Igneous rocks – are formed from volcanic magma or lava which has cooled and solidified.

Inclusions – are found within the crystal structure of gemstones. They can be large pieces of other crystals seen with the naked eye, or small cavities filled with solid, liquid or gas only visible under a microscope.

Iridescence – is due to interference of light in the internal structure of a stone, which causes white light to split into the spectral colours.

Isotropic – substances are those in which the properties, for example refraction, are the same in all directions.

Lustre – is the effect produced by light reflecting off the surface of a stone. Lustre may be vitreous (glass-like), adamantine (like a diamond), waxy, resinous, silky and so on.

Metamorphic rocks – are formed from *igneous* or *sedimentary* rocks that have been changed by high temperature and/or pressure.

Minerals – are naturally occurring inorganic substances that have a constant chemical composition and internal atomic structure.

Paste – is an artificial silica glass. It may be coloured and used to imitate a number of gemstones. It is easily scratched and worn.

Pegmatites – are *igneous* intrusions caused when residual liquids cool from magmas; gives an ideal growing region for crystals.

Pleochroism – occurs when a stone appears to be two (dichroic) or three (trichroic) different colours or shades of body colour when viewed from different directions.

Refraction – occurs as a ray of light passes from one medium to another of different density and is slowed and bent.

Refractive index (RI) – is a constant relationship between the angle at which light enters the gemstone and the angle of refraction.

Sedimentary rocks – are formed from the breakdown and deposition of *igneous* or *metamorphic* rocks.

Schiller (sheen) – in a gemstone is caused by reflection of light off the internal features of a stone.

Trichroism – see *Pleochroism*.

Twinning – occurs when a crystal grows in two different directions from one face.

FURTHER READING

Anderson, Basil W. and Jobbins, E.A., *Gem Testing,* Butterworth-Heinemann, 1990.

Balfour, Ian, *Famous Diamonds,* 2nd ed., NAG Press, 1992.

James, Duncan, *Old Jewellery,* Shire Publications Ltd, 1989.

Liddicoat, R., *Handbook of Gemstone Identification,* Gemmological Institute of America, 1977.

Mercer, Ian, *Crystals,* British Museum (Natural History)/Harvard University Press, 1990.

Nassau, Kurt, *Gems Made by Man,* Chilton Book Co, PA, 1980.

Nassau, Kurt, *Gemstone Enhancement,* Butterworths, 1984.

Read, Peter, *Gemmology,* Butterworth-Heinemann, 1991.

Read, Peter, *Dictionary of Gemmology,* Butterworths, 1988.

Schumann, Walter, *Gemstones of the World,* NAG Press Ltd, 1977.

Symes, Robert F., *Rock and Mineral,* Dorling Kindersley/British Museum (Natural History), 1988.

Symes, Robert F. and Harding, Roger R., *Crystal and Gem,* Dorling Kindersley/British Museum (Natural History), 1991.

Tait, Hugh (ed.), *Seven Thousand Years of Jewellery,* British Museum Publications, 1986.

Webster, Robert, *Gems – Their Sources, Descriptions and Identification,* Newnes-Butterworths & Co, 1983.

Webster, Robert and Jobbins, E.A., *Gemmologists Compendium,* NAG Press, 1986.

Woodward, Christine and Harding, Roger, *Gemstones,* British Museum (Natural History), 1988.

INDEX